Bank Asset and Liability Management

Bank Asset and Liability Management

The Hong Kong Institute of Bankers

WILEY

Other Wiley Editorial Offices
John Wiley & Sons, 111 River Street, Hoboken, NJ 07030, USA
John Wiley & Sons, The Atrium, Southern Gate, Chichester, West Sussex, PO19 8SQ, United Kingdom
John Wiley & Sons (Canada) Ltd., 5353 Dundas Street West, Suite 400, Toronto, Ontario, M9B 6HB, Canada
John Wiley & Sons Australia Ltd., 42 McDougall Street, Milton, Queensland 4064, Australia
Wiley-VCH, Boschstrasse 12, D-69469 Weinheim, Germany

Library of Congress Cataloging-in-Publication Data

Names: The Hong Kong Institute of Bankers, editor.
Title: Bank Asset and Liability Management / by The Hong Kong Institute of
   Bankers.
Description: Hoboken : Wiley, 2018. | Includes index. |
Identifiers: LCCN 2017049293 (print) | LCCN 2017050855 (ebook) | ISBN
   9780470827550 (pdf) | ISBN 9780470827567 (epub) | ISBN 9780470827536
   (paperback) | ISBN 9780470827550 (ePDF) | ISBN 9781119444497 (e-bk)
Subjects: LCSH: Asset-liability management. | Bank management. | BISAC:
   BUSINESS & ECONOMICS / Banks & Banking.
Classification: LCC HG1615.25 (ebook) | LCC HG1615.25 .B36 2017 (print) | DDC
   332.1068/1–dc23
LC record available at https://lccn.loc.gov/2017049293

Cover Design: Wiley
Cover Images: Stuttgart Fountain and Palace © iStockPhoto.com/Rolf Weschke; techno background © polygraphus/Shutterstock; marble © rusm/iStockphoto

Typeset in 11/14pt, ArnoPro by SPi Global, Chennai, India.

Printed in Singapore by Markono Print Media
10 9 8 7 6 5 4 3 2 1

Contents

Preface

'Bank Asset and Liability Management' (BALM) is a module within The Hong Kong Institute of Bankers (HKIB) curriculum of Treasury Management. As part of the Certified Banker qualifications structure, the syllabuses are tailor made for learning and development of a banking career in Hong Kong and Mainland China. This module is focused on developing the tools to manage assets and liabilities as well as providing practitioners with the knowledge necessary for strategic execution to ensure a safe and effective composition of assets and liabilities to support a bank's business model.

Why is this important? Bank treasury needs to be able to understand the complexity of market conditions. The implementation of an Asset and Liability Management (ALM) strategy set by the Asset and Liability Management Committee (ALCO) and bank management is closely linked to a bank's ability to implement effective risk controls. These range from interest rate risk to liquidity risk, which are among the eight inherent risks under constant vigilance of banks and financial institutions.

This book *Bank Asset and Liability Management* aims to equip banking professionals with the necessary knowledge and tools to understand the complexity of changing market conditions and to apply their learning to manage ALM and take advantage of emerging opportunities.

The Hong Kong economy has been resilient against international financial crisis and has earned the highest AAA sovereign credit rating from Standard & Poor's since 2010, thanks in part to the strong standard of governance and a well-regulated and capitalised banking sector. Due to the cross-border nature and the growing size of financial intermediation activities vis-à-vis the size of our economy, the banking sector must remain vigilant against future financial shock. Hong Kong is now the world's 4th largest foreign exchange centre. Strong BALM is critical to timely and sound execution, especially during times of crisis.

This book is divided into two parts and seven chapters that delve deeply into the subject matter. Every effort has been made to ensure that policies and regulations discussed in this book are up to date and current as at early 2016. Students are advised to keep themselves up to date from the web sites of HKIB, the regulator Hong Kong Monetary Authority (HKMA) and the Bank for International Settlements. At the time of writing, the regulations relating to Fundamental Review of Trading Book (FRTB) and OTC Derivatives are still evolving.

The first part of this book starts with a background discussion of bank asset and liability management. Chapter 1 considers the role of ALM in managing bank profitability, ensuring liquidity and drafting financial statements. Chapter 2 looks at the role of the Asset and Liability Management Committee (ALCO) that every bank has, including its role and functions and how it manages liquidity and funding risk. Chapter 3 dives right into the subject matter by considering how banks manage their assets and liabilities.

The second part of this book starts on Chapter 4 with a discussion of liquidity management, its definition and the steps banks take to ensure they always have enough liquidity to cover their liabilities. Chapter 5 takes a deep dive into a key facet of ALM, the management of interest rate risk. Chapter 6 takes a step back by considering how banks can manage ALM when market conditions are changing and risks grow larger.

The final chapter in this book brings the discussion to a practical conclusion by considering a series of case studies to illustrate how weaknesses in ALM can result in significant financial loss and even bankruptcy.

This book includes detailed explanations, summaries, tables and charts to help industry professionals develop a sound theoretical framework for their work in the field. Both students and working professionals can benefit from this detailed work produced in collaboration with some of Hong Kong's most prominent professionals. Aimed at banking practitioners, and designed as an essential tool to achieve learning outcomes, this book includes recommendations for additional reading. A 'Further reading' list can be found at the end of each chapter to help readers expand their knowledge of each subject.

A number of people were integral to the development of this work. Among them it is important to highlight Mr Peter Wong Wai Man for his valuable insight and review on the syllabus and content of this book. Mr Wong is also the Executive Board Member of the Treasury Markets Association and the former Regional Director and Treasurer of AIA and is now a director at PwC. There are many others whose contributions have been of particular significance in the preparation of this essential reference for banking professionals. The information provided in the collection of Hong Kong Monetary Authority publications has been instrumental in developing much of the book.

The preparation would not have been possible without the help, advice, support and encouragement of all these people and dozens more. We would like to extend our sincere thanks to them all.

The Hong Kong Institute of Bankers

PART 1

ASSET AND LIABILITY MANAGEMENT

1

Managing Bank Profitability

After studying this chapter, you should be able to:

1 Identify the process of asset and liability management (ALM) in the context of a bank's structure, regulations, financial statements and profits.

2 Describe how financial information on a balance sheet and a profit-and-loss statement can be used to analyse a bank.

3 Identify and explain the key sources of a bank's income, including net interest income and non-interest income.

4 Explain the general outlines of ALM as coordinated balance sheet management.

Introduction

Risk, return and capital provisions permeate all banking activity. Indeed, return on capital is a core objective of banking, and the degree of risk in an activity often determines a specified return on the capital used. How effectively a bank uses its capital often determines its success. That is why asset and liability management (ALM), which is overseen by the Asset and Liability Management Committee (ALCO), is so critical to all banking activities.

In this chapter, we put ALM in context by looking at bank structures and the regulations that proscribe them in different jurisdictions, bank financial statements, and evaluation of bank profits. Subsequent chapters will explore in greater detail the specifics of managing bank assets and liabilities, and of managing capital, including capital adequacy and planning. Later, we will also examine liquidity risk management and management of interest-rate risk, which are two areas that have a great impact on ALM.

Banks undertake all their activities on a foundation of capital, so understanding how capital is managed is of paramount importance to any prospective banking professionals. The differences between the banking book and the trading book and the various regulations that impact the movements of both for authorised institutions (AIs) in Hong Kong are examined in this chapter. Also considered are the basis of those regulations, often international agreements and accords.

The ultimate goal of ALM is to manage the risks associated with mismatches between assets and liabilities, risks that can be caused by, for example, issues with the liquidity that banks require to meet their liabilities or changes in interest rates, particularly given that banks tend to borrow short-term funds but lend long term. This chapter considers various ways to ensure profitability including return on equity, return on assets, net interest margin and net interest spread. At the same time, we consider how banks manage their balance sheets and distinguish between accounting and economic profit.

Structure and Regulation

Let us begin by examining bank structures and regulation in Hong Kong. Larger banks usually undertake a complex array of activities. These can be broadly grouped under two headings: commercial banking, which covers the more traditional deposits and loans business; and investment banking, which covers trading activity and fee-based income such as stock-exchange listing and mergers and acquisitions.

Banking Activities

As Figure 1.1 shows, the scope of banking is varied, ranging from everyday lending to such complex transactions as securitisation and trading of hybrid products. We will not discuss

FIGURE 1.1 Scope of banking activities

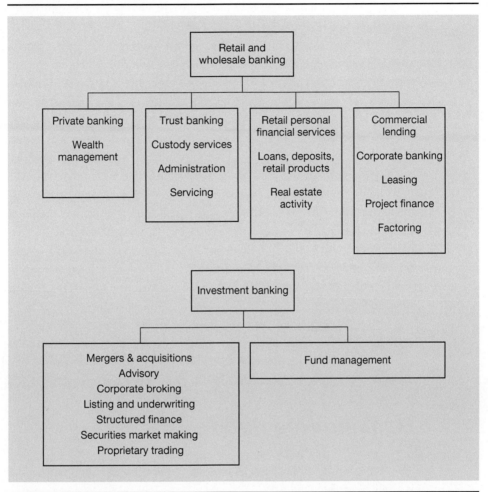

Source: Choudhry, Moorad (2007) *Bank Asset and Liability Management: Strategy, Trading, Analysis*. Singapore: John Wiley & Sons, p. 4.

the nature of these transactions in detail in this chapter, but a general knowledge of the basic products is useful as background. Most of them have been discussed in previous books in this series.

Because asset and liability management (ALM) is focused on the efficient management of banking capital, it has to concern itself with all banking operations—even if day-to-day contact between the ALM desk (which is responsible for the treasury and money-markets activities of the entire bank) and other parts of the bank is remote. In fact, we can draw a box with ALM in it around the whole of Figure 1.1.

This is not to say that the ALM function does all these activities, rather, that all the various activities represent assets and liabilities for the bank and one central function—ALM—is responsible for the coordinated management of these activities.

Capital is the equity of a bank. It enables a bank to continue operating and avoid insolvency in bad economic times and to give shareholders a good return on equity during normal and bull times.

The value of a bank's assets and liabilities tends to be far greater than the value of its capital. Even modest fluctuations (1% reduction) in the valuations of assets and liabilities can cause a significant (10% reduction) movement in capital. Capital management is thus a very important part of bank management. A bank organises its business into a banking book and a trading book.

The **banking book** records traditional banking activity such as deposits and loans. For accounting purposes, the banking book follows the accrual concept, which is accruing interest cash flows as they occur. There is generally no mark-to-market. The banking book holds assets for which corporate banking, retail banking as well as corporate centre are represented. The type of business activity dictates whether it is placed in the banking book, not the type of counterparty or the bank department involved.

Assets and liabilities in the banking book generate interest-rate and credit risks for the bank, and liquidity and term-mismatch ('gap') risk, which arises from either excess or shortage of cash. (Liquidity refers to the ease of transforming an asset into cash, or of raising funds in the market.)

The **trading book** records wholesale market activity, including market-making and proprietary trading. Assets on the trading book usually have a high turnover, and are marked-to-market daily. The counterparties to such activity can include other banks and financial institutions such as hedge funds, corporations and central banks.

Banking Regulation

Any discussion of ALM will not be complete without mentioning bank regulation. Banking is a highly regulated industry.

Hong Kong's banking regulator is the Hong Kong Monetary Authority (HKMA), which is responsible for maintaining monetary and banking stability. Its policy objectives are to maintain currency stability (the Hong Kong dollar is pegged to the US dollar); promote the safety and stability of the banking system; enhance the efficiency, integrity and development of the financial system; and promote Hong Kong's role as an international financial centre.

Bank regulators have the same objective in making sure banks do not take risks that are inappropriate for their size, capital, lines of business, ownership structure and other factors. The level of scrutiny and regulation has intensified in the wake of the 2008–2009 global financial crisis (GFC), when banks deemed too big to fail had to be bailed out in the US and Europe for fear their problems could cause a systemic collapse in the international financial system.

In the wake of the GFC, the US implemented the Troubled Asset Relief Program to help some of the largest banks in the country survive a liquidity crunch. The government poured capital into such giants as Citigroup and Bank of America. This capital went into banks that were deemed too big to fail. The need for such investments, however, highlighted gaps in the regulatory infrastructure in the US and Europe that opened the door to bank failures which would ultimately end up hurting consumers. Since the GFC, the Basel Committee on Banking Supervision (BCBS) of the Bank for International Settlements (BIS) has updated the Basel accords that act as the basis for regulatory structures in most countries around the world. Basel III, the latest iteration of the accords, is being implemented in stages and raises the amount of reserve capital that banks are expected to keep in hand to protect them against changes in the market.

How do bank regulators assess the operations of financial institutions to make sure they comply with the rules and best practice? Central banks have their own specific processes and procedures, including surprise on-site inspections, but there are similarities in the framework and principles of assessment. One framework is CAMEL, an acronym that takes the first letter of each of the five elements that bank regulators focus on when assessing banks:

- **C**apital adequacy
- **A**sset quality
- **M**anagement quality
- **E**arnings performance
- **L**iquidity.

Some supervisory authorities add an extra letter:

- **S**ensitivity to market risk.

We will discuss issues around capital adequacy in banks in Chapter 4 of this book.

Meeting Capital Requirements

Generally following the principles imbedded in Basel III, banks in Hong Kong are required by the HKMA to meet both capital adequacy and liquidity requirements. There are important differences between the two but, in broad strokes, capital adequacy refers to the bank's capital against the size of the overall balance sheet while liquidity requirements focus on the access to liquid assets that a bank might have on any given day.

The HKMA sets out a capital adequacy framework. The Hong Kong Banking Ordinance, which closely follows BCBS standards, includes a capital adequacy ratio that all banks and AIs should maintain, a 'supervisory review process to set and review individual institution's minimum capital adequacy ratio requirements' and a set of disclosure standards.[1]

---

[1]http://www.hkma.gov.hk/eng/key-functions/banking-stability/banking-policy-and-supervision/regulatory -framework.shtml.

The Capital Adequacy Ratio (CAR) is 'a ratio of a bank's capital base to its risk-weighted assets. The ratio is intended to be a measurement of a bank's capital position in respect of its exposures to credit risk, market risk and operational risk.'

Under Basel II, the HKMA required all banks to maintain a CAR of 8% but may increase the minimum ratio to as much as 16% under section 101 of the Banking Ordinance.[2] This is not to say that the HKMA can make arbitrary decisions. Rather, the Banking Ordinance gives the regulator some discretion, particularly when dealing with too-big-to-fail (TBTF) banks and the conditions under which the requirements can be changed are prescribed by law and not by the HKMA.

Every bank and AI is expected to calculate its own CAR based on the Banking (Capital) Rules included in the Banking Ordinance. From January 1, 2013, the capital adequacy rules started to change with the implementation of Basel III, which introduced reforms to the capital adequacy framework developed under Basel II. The Basel III changes are to be introduced in phases through 2019 and introduce a risk weight approach to the calculation of the CAR.

In the wake of Basel III, the HKMA moved to define CAR as a collective term to include three risk-weighted capital ratios, including a Common Equity Tier 1 (CET 1) capital ratio, a Tier 1 capital ratio and a total capital ratio. Although the percentages for each one changed progressively, through 2013 to 2015, the total capital ratio stayed flat at 8%.

Important as capital standards are for banks to remain solvent, they are only part of the picture. AIs in Hong Kong are also expected to meet minimum monthly average liquidity requirements. The rules are set out in the HKMA Supervisory Policy Manual.[3]

In January 2016, the BCBS introduced a series of standards for 'Minimum capital requirements for market risk' with differentiated requirements for the banking book and the trading book. The standards introduced a revised market risk framework that includes a revised internal models approach (MA) with a more rigorous approval process model, a revised standardised approach is more risk-sensitive, a move to an expected shortfall measure for risk under stress from value-at-risk (VaR), the incorporation of market illiquidity risk, and a revised line between the trading book and the banking book.[4]

The approach, which gives a risk weight to various activities depending on where they fall (banking book vs. trading book) and the amount of exposure to risk aims to replace standards for minimum capital requirements for market risk.

---

[2] Hong Kong Monetary Authority. 'Capital Adequacy Ratio'. Online. Accessed at http://www.hkma.gov.hk/gdbook/eng/c/capital_adequacy_ratio.shtml on 26 August 2016.

[3] Hong Kong Monetary Authority. 'Supervisory Policy Manual: Overview of Capital Adequacy Regime for Locally Incorporated Authorized Institutions'. Accessed at http://www.hkma.gov.hk/media/eng/doc/key-functions/banking-stability/supervisory-policy-manual/CA-G-1.pdf on 28 August 2016.

[4] Basel Committee on Banking Supervision. 'Minimum capital requirements for market risk'. January 2016.

Financial Statements

In assessing risks, regulatory compliance and profit opportunities, asset and liability management obviously needs to look at financial figures, both of the bank and occasionally of the major borrowers and organisations whose shares and bonds the bank owns. This data is contained in financial statements, which consist of a balance sheet and a profit-and-loss (p&l) report.

The assets on the balance sheet should equal the assets on a bank's asset and liability report. Receipts of revenue (such as interest and fees income) and payout of costs during a specified period are recorded in the p&l report or income statement.

Balance Sheet

The balance sheet, generally called the Statement of Financial Position in more up-to-date terminology, is a statement of a company's assets and liabilities as determined by accounting rules. Because it is a report released at a particular point in the company's business operations, it is already out of date by the time it is produced. Nonetheless, the balance sheet contains important information.

A bank's balance sheet usually is split into the following parts:

- loans and deposits or traditional bank business
- cash assets and short-term liabilities
- treasury and interbank assets and liabilities
- long-term assets, including fixed assets, shares in subsidiary companies, together with equity and Tier 2 capital, and long-term debt.

This is illustrated in Figure 1.2. The actual balance sheet of a retail or commercial bank will differ significantly from that of an investment bank due to the relative importance of their various business lines—cash and loans are key to retail banks while financial instruments and off-balance-sheet items are more important to investment banks. But the basic layout is similar for both types of institutions.

Income Statement

The profit-and-loss (p&l) report is a bank's income statement. It records all the bank's income and losses during a set period. It will show revenues that can be accounted for as net interest income, fees and commissions, or trading income.

The mix of these various sources of revenue is determined by the type of banking institution and its business lines. For example, a more 'traditional' retail or commercial

**FIGURE 1.2   An example of a balance sheet. From the 'Interim Report 2016'
(Hang Seng Bank)**

CONDENSED CONSOLIDATED FINANCIAL STATEMENTS
unaudited (continued)
(Expressed in millions of Hong Kong dollars)

Condensed Consolidated Balance Sheet	note	At 30 June 2016	At 30 June 2015	At 31 December 2013
ASSETS				
Cash and sight balances at central banks	18	18,938	40,317	10,118
Placings with and advances to banks	19	97,307	152,767	123,990
Trading assets	20	52,091	44,772	40,373
Financial assets designated at fair value	21	9,897	8,218	7,903
Derivative financial instruments	22	9,084	6,004	11,595
Reverse repurchase agreements - non-trading		–	1,904	–
Loans and advances to customers	23	678,442	673,022	688,946
Financial investments	24	375,403	328,198	372,272
Interest in associates	25	2,291	2,258	2,275
Investment properties	26	10,329	9,899	10,075
Premises, plant and equipment	27	26,074	25,664	26,186
Intangible assets	28	13,641	10,577	12,221
Other assets	29	27,870	27,838	28,475
Total assets		1,321,367	1,331,438	1,334,429
LIABILITIES AND EQUITY				
Liabilities				
Current, savings and other deposit accounts	30	951,545	947,495	959,228
Repurchase agreements - non-trading		1,761	3,032	2,315
Deposits from banks		14,159	13,964	18,780
Trading liabilities	31	58,156	77,543	62,917
Financial liabilities designated at fair value	32	4,004	4,027	3,994
Derivative financial instruments	22	11,590	5,877	9,988
Certificates of deposit and other debt securities in issue	33	6,416	7,738	5,191
Other liabilities	34	23,817	22,887	20,891
Liabilities under insurance contracts		104,425	96,986	101,817

FIGURE 1.2 *(Continued)*

CONDENSED CONSOLIDATED FINANCIAL STATEMENTS
unaudited (continued)
(Expressed in millions of Hong Kong dollars)

Condensed Consolidated Balance Sheet	note	At 30 June 2016	At 30 June 2015	At 31 December 2013
Current tax liabilities		1,546	1,906	185
Deferred tax liabilities		4,907	4,695	4,817
Subordinated liabilities	35	2,328	5,814	2,325
Total liabilities		1,184,654	1,191,964	1,192,448
Equity				
Share capital		9,658	9,658	9,658
Retained profits		100,615	102,085	105,363
Other equity instruments	37	6,981	6,981	6,981
Other reserves		19,459	20,750	19,979
Shareholders' funds	36	136,713	139,474	141,981
Total equity and liabilities		1,321,367	1,331,438	1,334,429

Source: Hang Seng Bank: 'Interim Report 2016' Accessed online at https://www.hangseng.com/cms/fin/file/statement/ir_2016
_en.pdf on 26 August 2016.

bank will depend far more on interest revenue than will an investment bank that engages in large-scale wholesale capital market transactions. Trading and fee income will form a larger share of an investment bank's revenue. Figure 1.3 shows the typical components of a retail bank's income statement.

Off-Balance-Sheet Items

Not all of a bank's financial information—and indeed of companies in general—is contained in financial statements. Off-balance-sheet transactions can be defined as 'contingent liabilities' of a bank and, as the name suggests, do not appear on a bank's balance sheet. These items are off the balance sheet because they refer to a future exposure contracted in the present time. They include interest-rate swaps, interest-rate options and currency options.

Off-balance-sheet items also refer to the following: direct credit substitutes, in which a bank substitutes its own credit for a third party (e.g. standby letters of credit; irrevocable letters of credit that guarantee repayment of commercial paper or tax-exempt securities); bankers' participation in sale and repurchase agreements; and asset sales with recourse against the seller.

FIGURE 1.3 Condensed Consolidated Income Statements (Hang Seng Bank)

CONDENSED CONSOLIDATED FINANCIAL STATEMENTS
unaudited
(Expressed in millions of Hong Kong dollars)

Condensed Consolidated Income Statement	note	Half-year ended 30 June 2016	Half-year ended 30 June 2015	Half-year ended 31 December 2015
Interest income	4	13,303	13,645	13,418
Interest expense	5	(2,300)	(3,204)	(2,694)
Net interest income		11,003	10,441	10,724
Fee income		3,776	4,638	3,986
Fee expense		(923)	(754)	(832)
Net fee income	6	2,853	3,884	3,154
Net trading income	7	455	1,377	653
Net incomes/(loss) from financial instruments designated at fair value	8	(30)	721	(839)
Dividend income	9	174	125	17
Net insurance premium income		5,608	6,247	3,598
Other operating income	10	1,788	1,880	2,039
Total operating income		21,851	24,675	19,346
Net insurance claims and benefits paid and movement in liabilities to policyholders		(6,634)	(8,125)	(4,843)
Net operating income before loan impairment charges and other credit risk provisions		15,217	16,550	14,503
Loan impairment charges and other credit risk provisions	11	(721)	(594)	(514)
Net operating income		14,496	15,956	13,989
Employee compensation and benefits		(2,441)	(2,537)	(2,356)
General and administrative expenses		(1,937)	(2,081)	(2,441)
Depreciation of premises, plant and equipment		(551)	(462)	(495)
Amortisation of intangible assets		(51)	(56)	(54)
Operating expenses	12	(4,980)	(5,136)	(5,346)
Impairment loss on intangible assets		—	—	(24)
Operating profit		9,516	10,820	8,619
Net gain on partial disposal of Industrial Bank		—	10,636	—
Net surplus/(deficit) on property revaluation		(77)	178	83
Share of profits from associates		60	86	66
Profit before tax		9,499	21,720	8,768
Tax expense	13	(1,494)	(1,672)	(1,322)
Profit for the period		8,005	20,048	7,446
Profit attributable to shareholders		8,005	20,048	7,446
(Figures in HK$)				
Earnings per share – basic and diluted	14	4.19	10.49	3.73

Source: Hang Seng Bank: 'Interim Report 2016' Accessed online at https://www.hangseng.com/cms/fin/file/statement/ir_2016_en.pdf on 26 August 2016.

Off-balance-sheet items therefore represent a liability for the bank that may be required to be honoured at some future date. In most cases, these items do not generate cash inflow or outflow at inception, unlike a cash transaction, but represent future exposure. Off-balance-sheet items only make it to the balance sheet when they are actually consummated, such as when a credit line is drawn on, for example. That represents a cash outflow and the transaction is thus recorded on the balance sheet.

Under the risk-based capital guidelines approved by most countries' banking regulators, banks are required to hold a portion of equity capital in reserve to meet contingent obligations in off-balance-sheet items. This portion is based on a risk-weighted scale that requires holding more capital in reserve for certain assets.

Evaluating Banks' Profits

Banks earn income from interest revenues, which are generated from lending and interest-earning assets, and non-interest revenues, which come from fees and commissions a bank charges its customers in return for the sale and provision of financial services and profits from trading of financial instruments.

Net interest income is interest revenue minus the cost of funds. Non-interest revenues consist of fees and commissions income and trading income. Retail banks typically focus on net interest income. Investment banks, on the other hand, derive most of their revenues from fees and commissions and from trading income.

Profit before tax is calculated by deducting expenses such as operating (non-interest) expenses, loan-loss provisions and trading losses (and ignoring tax) from core operating income. Net income is calculated by deducting tax from bank profit. Attributable income is calculated by deducting the amount due to minority interest from net income.

Net Interest Income

In retail banking, the ALM desk focuses primarily on the loan book, although it also concentrates on the bank's investment portfolio, which includes coupon receipts from money-market and bond-market assets as well as dividends from equity holdings.

The cost of funds is a key variable in generating overall net interest income. This cost represents the expense a bank incurs in order to maintain deposits and other liabilities on its balance sheet. The cost of funds includes the interest rate paid for liabilities (i.e. for deposits entrusted to the bank by its customers), which is determined by market rates as the benchmark.

The cost of funds is also determined by the bank's internal pricing decision as to how much margin it is willing to give up in order to attract and to retain deposits; and its credit rating, which determines how much the bank will pay in interest rates on its own bond issuances and other borrowings.

The cheapest source of funds is deposits, particularly cheque accounts that do not incur interest payments. (These are known as non-interest-bearing liabilities or NIBLs.) Despite intense competition, banks need to pay little or no interest at all on instant-access or short-term deposits.

This is one advantage that commercial banks have over investment banks, which usually do not have a retail deposit base. Other sources of finance for retail banks include capital markets (senior debt), wholesale markets (the interbank money market), securitised markets and covered bonds.

Net interest income is exposed to credit and market risks. It is vulnerable to fluctuations in interest rates and to the maturity profile of the bank's balance sheet, although such events are the exception rather than the norm.

However, in an environment of declining or low interest rates, a bank may experience negative net interest income, regardless of its asset-liability maturity profile. This is because a bank may not be able to pass on the rate cuts to depositors by lowering the interest rates it pays on deposits. If interest rates are too low, depositors may withdraw their money and put it into other vehicles such as equities.

An investment bank is subject to different forces as a result of the changes in interest rates. While it does not rely as much as commercial banks on net interest income, an investment bank's trading book is sensitive to rate changes. Equities and bonds typically rise in value; the opposite case usually happens when rates increase.

Fees and Commissions Income

Fees and commissions are generated from the sale and provision of financial services to customers. They are desirable revenue sources for banks because they are not exposed directly to market risk, unlike net interest income.

Fees and commissions are also attractive because they present banks with the opportunity to cross-sell new products and services to existing customers. Providing these services does not expose the bank to additional credit or market risk. Fee income represents diversification in a bank's revenue base. For banks, a positive aspect of providing bancassurance services is that they do not require banks to buy an insurance company—rather, a bank might receive commission from an insurance company from selling its products. This, for example, is what Standard Chartered Bank does with Prudential, receiving a commission from selling the insurance company's products to its customers.

Trading Income

Trading income refers to the capital gain earned from buying and selling financial instruments, including cash and derivatives. It can arise from:

- market-making business, which in theory is undertaken to meet client demands;
- proprietary business for the bank's own trading book.

Interest income earned while holding assets on the trading book should be considered as net interest income and not trading income.

Trading income is volatile. Even a record of consistent and sustained profit in trading is no guarantee against future losses stemming from a market correction or a wrong call on the financial markets. In fact, trading was the first banking activity to measure risk of losses on bank portfolio using value at risk methodology. There is another consideration that banks have to consider that is the Dodd-Frank Act from the US, which includes the Volcker Rule that limits banks from proprietary trading and restricts investments in hedge funds and private equity.

Operating Expenses

Operating expenses include human resources costs (salaries and wages and other personnel-related expenses) together with other operating costs such as rents and infrastructure maintenance, depreciation charges and goodwill. As discussed earlier, operating expenses are one of the items deducted from core operating income to calculate profit before tax, net income and attributable income.

Loan-Loss Provisions

Also deducted from core operating income to determine bank profit are loan-loss provisions. For a variety of reasons banks expect a percentage of their loans and other assets to suffer loss or become unrecoverable completely, these include borrower-specific problems, and serious economic recession such as the global downturn in 2008. Every year, they set aside provisions from reserves to cover these potential losses and account for them as a charge against revenues, i.e. as part of expenses.

The size of the provisions depends on the bank's own determination of the likely loan write-offs in the current portfolio and period, and in the future. In some instances, the regulator may direct that it set aside more in loan-loss provisions because the results of the CAMEL assessment demand it.

Some jurisdictions impose regulatory requirements on the minimum size of a provision. The latter funds a bank's loan-loss reserve and the reserve will grow if the provision made for expected credit losses is larger than the actual amount written off. If the bank decides subsequently that the size of the reserve exceeds current requirements, it may write back a portion of it, which then adds to bank profit for that year.

Basis of Capital Allocation

An important consideration is how to allocate risk-based capital and to develop capital allocation models. Risk-adjusted return on capital (RAROC) is a risk-based profitability framework to analyse risk-adjusted financial performance and develop a clear view of profitability across the business. The concept was first developed in the late 1970s and has evolved more into a measure of how well capital is being allocated with actual risk adjusted done on the basis of capital adequacy guidelines developed by the BCBS.

The basic formula for RAROC is simple:

$$RAROC = \frac{Expected\ return}{Economic\ capital}$$

Different institutions allocate their capital in different ways but the objectives of profitability, sustainability and risk control are the same. Some banks, such as Bank of America in the 1990s, developed capital allocation mechanisms that resembled the operations of capital markets. The original aim of RAROC frameworks was to measure risk in the credit portfolio of a bank and determine the adequate level of capital that is needed to allow a business unit to operate while limiting the exposure to loss of both depositors and debt-holders.[5]

RAROC systems are used to both manage capital and determine salaries while risk controls aim to influence the behaviour and activities of business units. Allocating capital among a growing number of activities at banks requires increasingly complex and sophisticated systems of capital allocation with the ultimate aim of measuring performance, allowing management to evaluate the performance and minimise risk. The systems can be used to determine how much capital is needed to support all banking activities: fee-generating, trading and traditional lending activities.

RAROC systems do this by assigning capital to various units while determining an appropriate rate of return that is adjusted for risk. The system can also be used to determine the economic value of each business unit and, ultimately, measure the contribution of every single business unit to the overall value of the bank.

One factor to consider is the contribution of each individual business to a bank's overall cash flow. This contribution is an important consideration when evaluating both the risk tolerance associated with that particular business and the amount of capital allocated to that business.

Measuring Bank Profitability

From the foregoing discussion, we know that bank profit depends on many factors, starting with the volume of interest and non-interest revenues and going on to the level of operating expenses, loan-loss provisions and other spending.

---

[5] James, Christopher (1996) 'RAROC Based Capital Budgeting and Performance Evaluation: A Case Study of Bank Capital Allocation'. The Wharton School, University of Pennsylvania Working Paper Series.

These elements are inter-related. If revenues increase, this does not automatically mean that bank profit will also rise. It is possible, in fact, for profit to fall because operating expenses have expanded even more and/or loan-loss provisions are much higher. Even more relevant for ALM is the important consideration that, while revenue might actually increase during a particular period, profits may fall due to rising interest rates that are not matched by loan prices. Conversely, even if revenues decrease, bank profits can still rise if operating expenses fall and/or provisions are lower.

A convenient way of tracking bank profitability is to look at a bank's profitability ratios. These include return on equity, return on assets, net interest margin and other measurements. Table 1.1 contains a summary of some of these ratios.

TABLE 1.1   Bank profitability ratios

Ratio	Calculation	Notes
Pre-tax ROE	Pre-tax income / Average shareholders' equity	Measures the pre-tax return on equity. A measure above 20% is viewed as above average and strong
ROE	Attributable net income / Average shareholders' equity	Measures return on equity. A measure above 10% is considered strong
ROA	Net income / Average assets	Measures return on assets. A measure above 1% is considered strong
Cost-income ratio	Non-interest costs / Total net revenues	Non-interest costs minus non-cash items such as goodwill or depreciation of intangible assets. The cost to produce one unit of net interest and non-interest income. The lower the ratio, the more efficient the bank
Net interest margin	Net interest income / Average earning assets	The difference between tax-equivalent yield on earning assets and the rate paid on funds to support those assets, divided by average earning assets
Loan loss provision	Loan-loss provision / Pre-provision, pre-tax income	The proportion of pre-tax income that is being absorbed by loan losses. This is the credit cost of conducting the business
Non-interest income	Non-interest income / Net revenues	Non-interest income includes service charges on deposits, trust fees, advisory fees, servicing fees, net trading profits from trading books, and commissions and fees from off-balance sheet items. Generally, the higher the ratio, the greater the bank's sensitivity to changes in interest rates

Source: Choudhry, Moorad (2007) *Bank Asset and Liability Management: Strategy, Trading, Analysis*. Singapore: John Wiley & Sons, p. 16.

Cost of Funds

The cost of funds (or cost of capital) generally refers to the cost that a bank or other type of company pays for the funds its uses in its activities, both debt and equity. Banks almost never use capital directly for investment or to lend to customers. Rather, a bank's capital is used to borrow cash that is then lent out to generate revenue. The capital is often a small base of shareholders' funds.[6] The cost of funds includes the cost of borrowing funds, which includes both the risk-free rate and a risk premium that often depends on the credit rating of a bank or particular instrument. It also includes the cost of equity, which is the return required by investors weighted for risk. The return of equity is often unknown but determined through comparisons with similar instruments or investments. The cost of debt and equity can be used to determine the weighted-average cost of capital (WACC), basically the cost that a bank faces for its operating funds.

The cost of funds is an important consideration for bank managers, particularly in regards to managing liquidity and ensuring that the bank always has access to enough liquidity to settle its obligations. This is the key function of liquidity managers and one of the most important considerations behind bank assets and liabilities management and one of the goals of effective credit management. An effective BALM strategy includes a risk-taking strategy that is ultimately profitable and is based on the real cost of funds.

To better understand and manage risk, banks often use a funds transfer pricing (FTP) mechanism that is key to mitigating risk and ensuring regulatory compliance. FTP has gained prominence since the global financial crisis of 2008, when it allowed banks to better navigate through the extreme volatility of the period. An effective FTP strategy allows banks to centralise the measurement and management of interest rate risk, consistently price the products of different business lines, set profitability targets for disparate business units and measure the profitability of each business unit regardless of volatile interest rate risk.

FTP can be difficult to implement despite the clear theoretical advantages it offers. For starters, the FTP strategy of a bank has to reflect its specific needs, so it must be developed specifically to meet its goals. Through an FTP framework, 'the costs of the risks included in ALM gaps, are explicitly charged to businesses, products, customers and centrally accounted for in the Treasury', writes Antonio Dalessandro, of University College London, in a 2013 paper. In other words, the internal funding structure of a bank is the basis for the criteria used to 'issue funding charges for the liquidity risk placed on the balance sheet by each business line'.[7]

---

[6]Dalessandro, Antonio (2013) 'Effective Strategies for Assets and Liabilities Management'. University College London. Available online through the Social Science Research Network.

[7]Ibid, pp. 13–14.

Return on Equity (ROE)

A common way to measure a bank's profitability is to examine its return on equity. ROE is calculated using this formula:

$$\frac{\text{Net income}}{\text{Shareholders' equity}}$$

A bank will typically have a target ROE as part of its management objectives. Its strategy and operations, therefore, are oriented towards achieving this ROE. Before the 2008 global financial crisis, for example, the target ROE in the US was typically 15% or higher, with the targets of investment banks at 20% or more. The ROE targets have now been reduced (e.g. HSBC target is 10%) in line with higher regulatory capital requirement and various compliance costs.

Ideally, ROE targets should reflect the relative risk of a bank's different business activities. However, market exuberance and shareholder demands may occasionally force management to set ROE objectives too high: the bank may take on more risks in the form of large loans to untested borrowers, for example, or trading positions in highly risky financial instruments in order to meet those targets.

Return on Assets

Another common measure of a bank's performance is return on assets (ROA). This is calculated as follows:

$$\frac{\text{Net income (Interest income + fees)}}{\text{Asset value}}$$

ROA is traditionally the ratio used to measure a bank's efficiency. The higher the ratio, the more efficient the bank is in making productive use of its assets. A ROA of better than 1% is considered as a strong performance.

ROA is especially useful for assessing profitability when the bank is focused on building asset size, as financial institutions were doing during the mergers and acquisitions spree of the 1980s. If ROA does not improve, even as the bank piles on new assets, that may be an indication that the assets being acquired are not worth the financial outlay, or that they are not being utilised as efficiently as they should be.

When banks were mostly focused on lending and had not yet developed fee-based and trading businesses, ROA was considered as important as ROE in measuring bank profitability. However, this changed when the Bank for International Settlements issued its recommendation for banks to maintain a capital adequacy ratio of 8%, with the attendant calculation based on risk-weighting of bank assets. ROA comparisons among banks became somewhat misleading because ROA does not adjust for differences in risk weightings.

ROA and, to a certain extent, even ROE and p&l reports are straightforward calculations of absolute values. Because they do not adjust for relative risk exposure, they cannot be compared too closely with the equivalent figures of another bank. This is because the risk exposure and the specific type of business activity differ from one financial institution to another.

Net Interest Margin

Net interest margin can also help in bank analysis. Net interest income is calculated using this formula:

$$\frac{\text{Net interest income}}{\text{Average earning assets}}$$

The cost of funds has a great impact on a bank's net interest margin. In general, a bank with a high proportion of non-interest bearing liabilities has a low cost of funding, while one with a high proportion of interest-paying deposits has a high cost of funding.

As such, a bank with a strong unsecured lending franchise should seek significantly higher yields than one investing in secured mortgage loans. In other words, the risk profile of the assets that generate yields for the bank should be taken into account. A high net interest margin is desirable, but it should be appropriate to the risks incurred in holding an asset.

Basically, another name for this is net interest spread, which is the percentage point difference between the interest rate a bank earns on its assets and the interest rate it pays on its liabilities (e.g. bank deposits). It is a good indicator of the profitability of an institution's interest income, and is thus a useful benchmark in asset and liability management.

Balance Sheet Management

As discussed earlier, a bank's assets and liabilities are contained in its balance sheet. Asset and liability management, therefore, is in large part concerned with balance sheet management with the aim of maximising profitability within the constraints of regulations and risks. As the Society of Actuaries defines it, 'ALM is the ongoing process of formulating, implementing, monitoring and revising strategies related to assets and liabilities to achieve the financial objectives for a given set of risk tolerances and constraints.'

The importance and functions of ALM can be viewed in terms of the following three-stage approach to balance sheet management as presented in Table 1.2:

- **Stage I** reflects a general approach that focuses on coordinated management of a bank's assets, liabilities, capital and off-balance-sheet activities.

TABLE 1.2   A three-stage view of asset and liability management

Stage I (General)

Asset management	Liability management
	Capital management
Off-balance-sheet activities (OBSAs)	OBSAs

Stage II (Specific)

Reserve-position management	Liability management, LM ('purchased funds')
Liquidity management	Reserve-position LM (Federal Funds)
Investment/securities management	Generalised or loan-position LM (CDs)
Loan management	Long-term debt management (notes and debentures)
Fixed-asset management ('bricks and mortar')	Capital management (common equity)
OBSAs	OBSAs (e.g. interest-rate derivatives, IRDs)

Stage III (Balance sheet generates the income–expense statement, given interest rates and prices)

Profit = interest revenue – interest expenses – provision for loan loss + non-interest revenue – non-interest expenses – taxes

Free cash flow = cash from operations + balance sheet sources – balance sheet uses

Source: HKIB.

- **Stage II** identifies specific components of a bank's balance sheet used in coordinating overall portfolio management. The process in Stage II focuses on planning, directing and controlling the levels, changes, and mixes of the various on- and off-balance-sheet accounts, which generate the bank's income and expense statement.
- **Stage III** shows that, given interest rate and prices, a bank's balance sheet generates its income–expense statement and free cash flow.

Except for the management of fixed physical assets, all of a bank's earning assets play a crucial role in asset and liability management. The interest rate, volumes and mixes of these asset categories are the critical elements of the asset management component of ALM. A bank's asset management can thus be described in terms of reserves, liquidity, investment securities and loans.

An important distinction is between assets that are rate sensitive and those that are not rate sensitive. This sensitivity can be described in terms of the effective time to re-pricing or duration. By definition, reserves and other liquid assets re-price quickly; long-term, fixed rate securities and loans do not.

The liquidity management (LM) aspect of ALM can be viewed in terms of two functions. First, reserve-position LM focuses on the use of short-term instruments to meet deposit withdrawals or to temporarily meet loan demand. *Repurchase agreements* (securities sold under agreement to repurchase and known as 'repos' or 'RP') and *purchase of Federal Funds* (excess reserves traded overnight among banks) are the basic instruments of reserve-position LM.

This LM method generates short-term sources of funds to complement liquidity stored in a bank's balance sheet. The technique, which permits a bank to hold higher-yielding, less-liquid assets, mainly affects the composition of a bank's balance sheet. However, a bank that attempts to use Federal Funds to finance a permanent expansion of its assets incurs substantial liquidity risk. Failure to maintain its creditworthiness will jeopardise the bank's ability to roll over the funds.

The second type of LM is generalised or loan-position LM. It focuses on a permanent expansion of a bank's balance sheet to meet profitable investment opportunities, especially customer loan demand. Large certificates of deposits (CDs) are the primary instrument of this technique. Large, creditworthy banks purchase such funds in either domestic or international money markets. Investors may sell these large CDs in secondary markets, which makes them negotiable instruments.

Funds gathered in local markets, mainly by smaller banks, are known as core deposits. To tap funds outside local markets, banks can use the technique of brokering deposits whereby a large, retail brokerage firm such as Merrill Lynch sell the banks' CDs. The basic differences between purchased funds and core deposits are the higher cost and greater variability of purchased funds ('hot money') compared to core deposits.

Both types of LM involve an active rather than a passive approach to attracting sources of bank funding. The maturity, risk, and other characteristics of the underlying instruments distinguish the two approaches. As with bank assets, an important distinction is between liabilities that are rate-sensitive and those that are not rate-sensitive. This sensitivity also can be described in terms of the effective time to re-pricing or duration. By definition, Federal funds, purchased repos and money-market accounts re-price quickly, while longer term, fixed rate CDs do not re-price as quickly.

Because of the short-term nature of asset and liability management, long-term debt and equity capital are not day-to-day instruments of ALM. They are included in Table 1.2 for the purpose of giving a complete picture of a bank's balance sheet. Nevertheless, to the extent that a bank raises additional long-term sources of funds, it can lengthen its average asset maturity and, all other things being equal and assuming a positively shaped yield curve, increase its interest revenue.

Stage III of coordinated bank balance sheet management shows a bank's income–expense statement (and free cash flow) as generated by its on- and off-balance-sheet activities, given interest rate and prices. This stage highlights the policies bankers need to achieve their objectives.

These policies, which flow from the abbreviated income–expense statement shown in Stage III, focus on:

- spread management
- loan quality

- generating fee income and service charges
- control of non-interest operating expenses
- tax management
- capital adequacy
- hedging practices.

To summarise, ALM involves a global or general approach (Stage I) that requires coordination of the various specific functions (Stage II). The process in Stage II focuses on planning, directing and controlling the levels, changes, and mixes of the various on- and off-balance-sheet accounts, which generate the bank's income and expense statement (Stage III).

Accounting Profit vs Economic Profit

In considering the management of assets and liabilities and the various approaches to ALM, it is also important to keep in mind the difference between accounting profits and economic profits, which can be significant. A bank that is profitable on paper may actually not be profitable in reality as the risk factors and the opportunity costs of not doing other business are taken into account. Accounting profits, then, are total earnings calculated based on accounting principles and typically exclude costs of doing business such as depreciation, interest and taxes.

Economic profits are actual, real life profits: the revenue derived from the sale of products and services and the opportunity costs of the inputs that went into producing those outputs. Another name for economic profit is 'economic value added' (EVA). When calculating economic profits, opportunity costs have to be deducted from revenues because opportunity costs are other returns that were foregone in using specific inputs. Economic profits for banks are determined using a ratio such as RAROC which considers expected loss, which is a risk measure of the degree of riskiness of the loan portfolio it puts in its balance sheet. RAROC has the benefit of taking into account risk factors and costs.

RAROC is defined as:

$$= \frac{\text{Expected profit}}{\text{Economic capital}}$$

$$= \frac{(\text{Profit} - \text{expected loss} - \text{fees})}{\text{Economic capital}}$$

There is a difference between accounting profit and economic profit, which leads to a dilemma when it comes to managing BALM. Should a bank maximise profit by chasing after higher asset yield businesses or chase after more volume business?

In general, accounting profits are higher than economic profits, not only because they don't take into account some actual costs but also because they fail to account for a number of other costs such as opportunity costs. It is entirely possible to have accounting profits while incurring economic losses. Imagine a bank invests HKD1 million to start a new line of business that earns HKD1.2 million in one year. The accounting profit would be the HKD0.2 million. Imagine, however, that to start that new line of business the bank had to divert resources from another line of business that would have earned the bank HKD0.5 million without any investment. So, what was an accounting profit then becomes an economic loss because of the opportunity cost of HKD0.3 calculated by subtracting the HKD1 million in investment and HKD0.5 million in lost profits from the HKD1.2 million that the new business earned.

The concept of expected loss has increased in popularity. In the latest accounting rules for financial instruments (HKFRS 9) to be effective in 2018, banks are required to adopt expected credit loss instead of incurred loss in determining the amount of loan impairment.

These are important considerations for bank management but ALM is less concerned with final profitability and more with the allocation of capital. ALM, in essence, is the structure that links risk management and regulatory compliance to profitability. It is useful to think of it as an upward-pointing triangle with risk management on one side, regulatory compliance on the other and profitability at the top point of intersection. ALM is everything in between.

Summary

- Asset and Liability Management (ALM) concerns itself with all banking operations, even if day-to-day contact between the ALM desk and other parts of the bank is remote.
- Capital is the equity of a bank, and the bedrock on which it undertakes all its activities. The value of a bank's assets and liabilities tends to be far greater than the value of capital and even a modest fluctuation in those values can significantly erode capital.
- The banking regulator in Hong Kong is the Hong Kong Monetary Authority (HKMA). The policy objectives of the HKMA are to maintain currency stability, promote the safety and stability of the banking system and enhance the financial system of the Special Administrative Region (SAR). In Mainland China, banks are regulated by the China Banking Regulatory Commission.
- The banking book records traditional banking activity such as deposits and loans. The trading book records wholesale market activity, including market making and proprietary trading.
- CAMEL is an internationally recognised bank-rating system that assesses an institution's: Capital adequacy, Asset quality, Management, Earnings and Liquidity. Each factor is assigned a score in ascending order of concern, ranging from 1 (best, i.e. of least concern) to 5 (worst, i.e. of most concern).
- Hong Kong's banking regulations, capital and liquidity requirements are generally based on the Basel Accords of the Basel Committee on Banking Supervision (BCBS)

that is part of the Bank for International Settlements (BIS). Basel III is currently being implemented in stages.

- A bank's financial statements consist of a balance sheet and a profit-and-loss (p&l) report. The balance sheet is a statement of a bank's assets and liabilities as determined by accounting rules. The p&l report records all the bank's income and losses during a set period.

- Off-balance-sheet items refer to a bank's future exposure or contracted liabilities. These items include interest-rate swaps, interest-rate options and currency options and, as the name indicates, do not appear on the balance sheet.

- Banks generate cash through interest revenues, which come from lending and interest-earning assets, and non-interest revenues, which come from the fees and commissions a bank charges its customers in return for the sale and provision of financial services and from profits from the trading of financial instruments.

- Net interest income is interest revenue minus the cost of funds. Retail banks typically focus on net interest income. Investment banks, on the other hand, derive most of their revenues from fees and commissions and from trading income.

- Return on Equity (ROE) and Return on Assets (ROA) are two ratios that can be used to measure a bank's profitability and effectiveness. ROE is usually part of a bank's strategy, and management objectives set explicit ROE targets. ROA is calculated as current income over asset value.

- The importance and functions of ALM can be viewed in terms of a three-stage approach to balance sheet management. Stage I reflects a general approach that focuses on coordinated management of assets, liabilities, capital and off-balance-sheet activities. Stage II focuses on planning, directing and controlling the levels, changes, and mixes of the various on- and off-balance-sheet accounts, which generate the bank's income and expense statement (Stage III).

- Accounting profits is the profit, on paper, earned by a bank or operation and does not take into account a number of business costs such as taxes, depreciation or opportunity cost. Economic profit takes all these costs into account. It is possible to have an accounting profit but an economic loss.

Key Terms

Accounting profit	Economic value added
Asset and liability management (ALM)	Funds transfer pricing (FTP)
Asset and Liability Management	Liquidity management (LM)
Committee (ALCO)	Net interest income (NII)
Banking book	Net interest margin (NIM)
CAMEL(S)	Net interest spread
Economic profit	Non-interest-bearing liability (NIBL)

Off-balance-sheet instruments
Profit-and-loss (p&l)
Return on assets (ROA)
Return on equity (ROE)

Risk-adjusted return on capital (RAROC)
Trading book
Trading income

Review Questions

1. A bank typically has a banking book and a trading book. Why is there a need for these two books and what are the differences between them?
2. Bank A is a retail bank in Hong Kong, while Bank B is the Hong Kong operation of a US investment bank. What are the likely sources of each bank's earnings, and what would be the reasons for the difference?
3. Explain how a bank's profitability can be analysed using financial information in a balance sheet and a profit-and-loss report, as well as the ratios generated from those numbers.
4. How is the composite interest rate in Hong Kong derived? Assuming all assets of a bank are prime-based, what will be the impact on net interest spread if the bank prices the cost of funding according to the composite rate?
5. What is the three-stage approach for asset and liability management to use in managing the balance sheet?

Further Reading

Adam, Alexandre (2007) *Handbook of Asset and Liability Management: From Models to Optimal Return Strategies*. Chichester: John Wiley & Sons.

Basel Committee on Banking Supervision. 'Minimum capital requirements for market risk'. January 2016.

Choudhry, Moorad (2007) *Bank Asset and Liability Management: Strategy, Trading, Analysis*. Singapore: John Wiley & Sons (Asia) Pte Ltd.

Hong Kong Monetary Authority. http://www.info.gov.hk/hkma/.

_____. The Composite Interest Rate of Hong Kong – A New Data Series. 12 April 2010. http://www.info.gov.hk/hkma/eng/research/RM26-2005.pdf.

Koch, Timothy W. and MacDonald, Scott S. (2010) *Bank Management* (7th edn). United States: South-Western Cengage Learning.

CHAPTER 2

Asset and Liability Management Committee (ALCO)

After studying this chapter, you should be able to:

1 Describe the functions of an Asset and Liability Management Committee (ALCO) and explore how various financial reports enable the committee to review ALM strategies.

2 Identify and evaluate the strategies for a bank to manage its liquid assets such as cash, securities and loans.

3 Compare the different liabilities that a bank carries, and understand why these are critical to a bank's operations.

4 Identify liquidity and funding risks, and describe ways to mitigate these risks.

Introduction

This chapter examines a critical part of a bank's operations—management of its assets and liabilities. It explores the roles of the bank's ALM desk and Asset and Liability Management Committee, and how these two units work to mitigate the risks of holding assets and liabilities.

We also look at ALM approaches such as management of liquid assets, including cash, securities and loans and explore a bank's different liabilities and the sources of funds for them. This chapter also touches upon the matched-book technique, gap management and securitisation as ALM methods.

ALCO Role and Functions

The Asset and Liability Management Committee, commonly known as ALCO, is an important structure put in place in a bank to effectively manage its assets and liabilities so that the potential profits are balanced out against the risks that the bank takes. ALCOs can be set up at local, regional or global levels, depending on the operational scale of the bank. The committee should have representation from both the assets and liabilities sides of the business, and in particular from those personnel who take decisions that affect assets and liabilities. The ALCO usually has a specific remit to oversee all aspects of ALM, from the front-office money market function to back-office operations and middle-office reporting and risk management.

The committee includes the bank's senior management, such as the chief executive officer or managing director, treasurer, chief financial officer, chief operating officer, chief credit officer, and heads of consumer banking and corporate banking. The exact composition of the ALCO may vary by institution, but the executives usually present are the heads of treasury, trading and risk management. Representatives from the credit committee and loan syndication may also be present.

Specifically, the ALCO sets targets for net interest income, devises strategies to achieve these targets, and shapes a bank's balance sheet under an adequate risk management framework and regulatory compliance limits. Such limits include liquidity ratios, capital adequacy ratio and leverage ratio. The ALCO is responsible for overseeing operations to ensure that the bank manages its funds adequately in order to meet profitability objectives, even as it keeps interest-rate and liquidity risks in check.

Other ALCO functions depend on a bank's size and focus. The ALCO could devise appropriate strategies to address cash-flow needs reflected in scenario analysis, conduct interest-rate projections, and assess credit, liquidity and interest-rate risks.

The HKMA says the ALCO is an 'important feature in the effective management of the assets and liabilities' of a bank. Its most fundamental function is to oversee the operations as they relate to interest rate and liquidity risk and ensure that a bank or financial institution has enough liquidity in hand at all times to cover its obligations. These functions call for some heavyweight experience and insight. In general, the ALCO includes senior staff such as the chief executive, chief financial officers, treasurer, chief credit officer and the bank officer in charge of deposit-taking; various division heads may also take part.

Asset and Liability Management

As we mentioned earlier, the ALCO is responsible for setting and implementing ALM policy, including hedging. The Treasury desk or another dedicated function may undertake the actual ALM under the ALCO's leadership.

In traditional commercial banks, the ALM desk reports regularly to the ALCO on the bank's risk exposure. The ALCO deliberates on the report at regular meetings, whose frequency depends on the type of institution but is usually monthly. The main points in the report include variations in interest income, the areas experiencing income fluctuations, and the latest short-term income projections. The ALM report links these three strands across the group and to each individual business line. In other words, it considers the macro-level factors driving variations in interest income as well as specific desk-level factors. The former includes changes in the yield curve, while the latter includes new business and customer behaviour, among other factors.

A typical ALCO meeting will discuss the following action points:

- **Management reporting.** Various management reports are analysed and either accepted or have items flagged for action. Topics for consideration could cover lending margins, interest income, variance from the last projection and future business. Current business policies on loans and portfolio management are reviewed and either continued or adjusted.
- **Business planning.** Existing asset (and liability) books are reviewed and future business direction outlined. Towards this end, the performance of existing business is analysed, particularly with regard to return on capital. The risk–reward profile of the asset portfolio is analysed with the aim of continuing or modifying various lines of business. Proposals for new business are discussed and, if approved in principle, are moved to the next stage.
- **Hedging policy review.** The ALCO meeting reviews and resets (if necessary) the bank's overall hedging policy. It considers risk exposure, existing risk limits and the use of hedging instruments, including derivatives. Hedging policy takes into account the levels of cash book revenue and current market volatility, as well as the overall cost of hedging. On occasion, certain exposures may be left un-hedged because hedging costs would be prohibitive. The ALCO decides hedging policy in coordination with overall funding and liquidity policy.
- **Regulatory compliance status.** Another important consideration for the ALCO is ongoing regulatory compliance. Regulatory compliance has emerged as a significant activity for banks, with more know-your-customer and ALM requirements on top of more stringent capital requirements that banks have to meet.

Another important consideration of market risk is value-at-risk (VaR), which is used to calculate the potential impact not of a risk but of a risk event. VaR is an important consideration for the ALCO in its decision-making process. VaR is a measure of the worst expected loss that a bank may suffer over a specific period of time, under normal market conditions and a specified level of confidence. Another way of looking at VaR is that it is the expected loss of a portfolio over a specified time period for a set level of probability. For example, if a daily VaR is stated as $100,000 to a 95% level of confidence, this means that during the day there is only a 5% chance that the loss the next day will be greater than $100,000. The most commonly used VaR models assume that the prices of assets in the financial markets follow a normal distribution.

Although Basel III rules are moving away from using VaR, there are a number of advantages to using this approach, particularly as a tool in decision-making. These advantages include letting senior management set overall risk targets, managing risk capital

FIGURE 2.1   Reporting for the ALCO

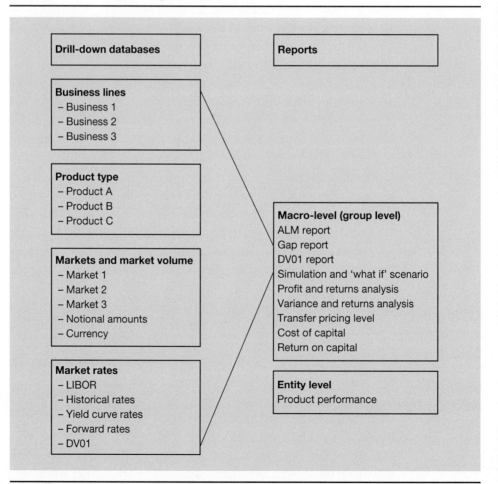

Source: Choudhry, Moorad (2007) *Bank Asset and Liability Management: Strategy, Trading, Analysis*. Singapore: John Wiley & Sons, p. 331.

allocation, facilitate reporting and disclosure, facilitate the implementation of hedging strategies and evaluate the performance of both assets and individuals. On the other hand, VaR does not provide a consistent method to measure risk and only measures risks that can be captured through quantitative techniques because it cannot measure political, liquidity, personnel, regulatory or operational risks nor can it effectively measure potential losses associated with a tail event.

Reporting for the ALCO

The ALCO depends upon reports from the ALM or Treasury desks. The main overall report shows the composition of the bank's ALM book; others examine specific business lines and their returns on capital. They break down aggregate levels of revenue and risk by business line, and some also drill down by product type. Yet others consider the gap, gap risk, VaR or DV01 (interest risk) and credit risk. The reports also practice scenario planning, looking at probable performance under various macro- and micro-level market conditions. Figure 2.1 illustrates the overall reporting system for the ALCO.

FIGURE 2.2 Expected liquidity and interest-rate gap: a snapshot profile

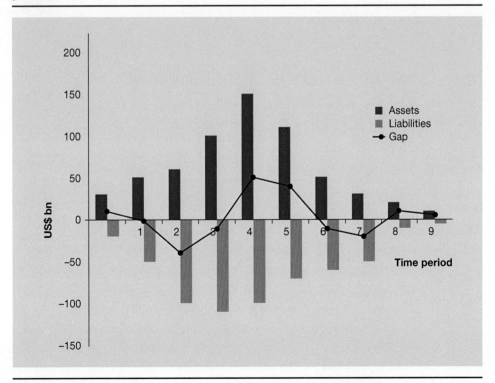

Source: Choudhry, Moorad (2007) *Bank Asset and Liability Management: Strategy, Trading, Analysis*. Singapore: John Wiley & Sons, p. 332.

FIGURE 2.3   ALM breakdowns by product (or market) segment

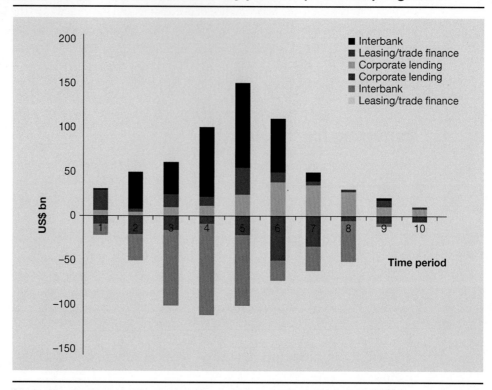

Source: Choudhry, Moorad (2007) *Bank Asset and Liability Management: Strategy, Trading, Analysis*. Singapore: John Wiley & Sons, p. 333.

Examples of reports for the ALCO

Let us sample the types of reports provided to the ALCO for its review. The examples are general, and actual reports would be determined by the type of institution reviewed and its business lines.

- **Expected liquidity and interest-rate gap.** The first example, Figure 2.2, depicts a typical dynamic gap with projected interest-rate gaps based on a current snapshot profile. This report shows future funding requirements, on which the ALCO can base its direction for future interest-rate levels. Because it shows the volume of assets, the report also illustrates the points where revenue can be vulnerable to falling interest rates. It can assist the ALCO to judge if interest income may be affected adversely, and accordingly decide on hedging. The x axis shows time buckets from overnight out to two years or beyond. Banks use different time buckets to suit their own requirements.
- **ALM breakdowns by product (or market) segment.** The second example, Figure 2.3, shows the same report with a breakdown by product (or market). We use a hypothetical sample of different business lines. This format reveals to the ALCO which assets and liabilities are producing the gaps, thereby showing if the products (or markets) fit into the bank's overall policy. Moreover, the report illustrates the

proportion of total assets represented by each business line, thereby determining which line has the greatest forward-funding requirement. This can enable the ALCO to adjust its policy accordingly.

- **ALM breakdowns by type of interest rate.** The third example, Figure 2.4, is the same report as Figure 2.3 but with the breakdown by type of interest rate, fixed or variable. In another variation of this report, the breakdown is by income and margin, again separated into business lines or markets.
- **Asset profile volume and average income spread.** The fourth example, Figure 2.5, is another type of income report, which illustrates the volumes and income spread by business line. The spread is shown in basis points and is an average for that time bucket (across all loans and deposits for that bucket). The volumes are those reported in the main ALM report (Figure 2.2), but with the margin contribution per time period.
- **Business lines and average income spread.** As we might expect, the spread levels per product across time are roughly similar. They will differ more markedly by product line as shown in Figure 2.6, which shows the performance of each business line. In general, the ALCO will prefer low volumes and high margin as a combination, because lower volumes consume less capital. However, some significant high-volume business (such as interbank money market operations) operates at a relatively low margin.

FIGURE 2.4 ALM breakdowns by type of interest rate

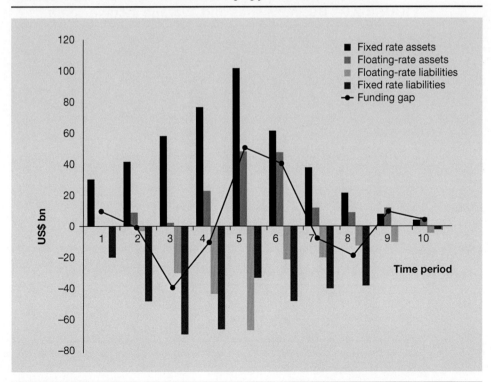

Source: Choudhry, Moorad (2007) *Bank Asset and Liability Management: Strategy, Trading, Analysis.* Singapore: John Wiley & Sons, p. 334.

FIGURE 2.5   Asset profile volume and average income spread

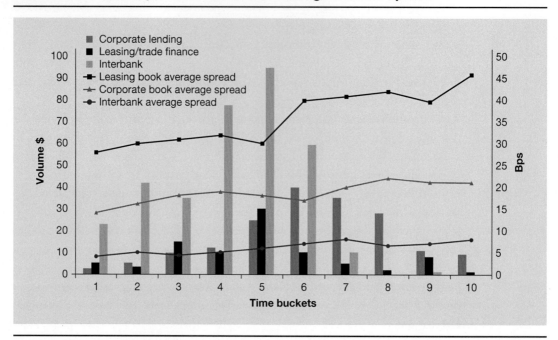

Source: Choudhry, Moorad (2007) *Bank Asset and Liability Management: Strategy, Trading, Analysis*. Singapore: John Wiley & Sons, p. 335.

FIGURE 2.6   Business lines and average income spread

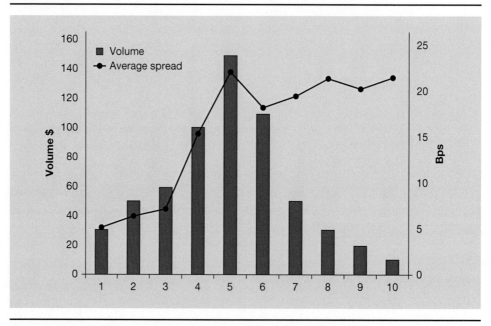

Source: Choudhry, Moorad (2007) *Bank Asset and Liability Management: Strategy, Trading, Analysis*. Singapore: John Wiley & Sons, p. 336.

Liquidity and Funding Risk Management

As discussed in Chapter 1, ALM seeks to mitigate two main dangers in banking: interest-rate risk and liquidity risk. ALM is conducted mainly at an overview, balance-sheet level, and risks are managed at an aggregate, group level. The reason? A viable banking business cannot be run by leaving the management of interest rate and liquidity risk to individual operating levels.

Liquidity Risk

Let us look first at liquidity risk. Liquidity is of critical importance to a bank. It establishes the bank's ability to fund new assets and lower its liabilities. It is the bank's protection against expected and unexpected fluctuations in assets and liabilities.

Liquidity risk therefore is unwelcome to the bank. It occurs on the liability side when debt-holders such as depositors withdraw their money. Liquidity risk arises from normal banking operations, i.e. it exists irrespective of the type of funding gap, be it excess assets over liabilities for any particular time bucket, or an excess of liabilities over assets.

The liquidity risk in itself generates interest-rate risk, due to the uncertainty of future interest rates. This can be managed through hedging.

Another issue to consider is fund transfer pricing (FTP) practices, which can lead to weaknesses in funding and add to liquidity risk. FTP is a useful tool to use in BALM. FTP allocates funding and contingent liquidity risks to business lines, products or activities and, in turn, influences the volume and terms of these business lines. FTP can lead to more resilient and sustainable business models but it can also be the cause of a misalignment of risk-taking incentives between individual business lines and the bank as a whole. This can, in turn, lead to a misallocation of resources. Such a misallocation can lead to excessive risk-taking, particularly in new business lines. There are a number of examples of this, such as unnecessary or excessive off-balance-sheet commitments or growth in on-balance-sheet assets due to mispriced funding.[1]

Funding Risk

A bank should weigh the costs of each type of funding against its risk. There is the risk of withdrawal associated with liabilities, and the risk of loss in interest rate changes. Besides traditional sources, a bank can explore avenues of financing such as securitisation and service-fee income.

Other funding risks are related to liquidity risk and to maturity mismatch of assets and liabilities. Maturity mismatch may result in a shortage of funds when longer-term

---

[1] Federal Deposit Insurance Corporation. 'Interagency Guidance on Funds Transfer Pricing Related to Funding and Contingent Liquidity Risks.' March 1, 2016. Accessed online on September 20, 2016 at https://www.federalreserve.gov/bankinforeg/srletters/sr1603a1.pdf.

assets cannot be liquidated to provide funds for withdrawal of shorter-term liabilities. Low liquidity of assets and high concentration of loans in particular sectors also lead to funding risks.

Matched-Book Approach

The simplest way to manage liquidity risk and interest-rate risk is the matched-book approach, also known as cash-flow matching. This is actually very rare in practice, even among conservative institutions. In the matched-book approach, assets and liabilities, and their time profiles, are matched as closely as possible. This includes allowing for the amortisation of assets.[2]

Not only are maturities and time profiles matched, but so also is the interest-rate basis for both assets and liabilities (i.e. fixed loans to fund fixed-rate assets, and the same for floating-rate assets and liabilities). Floating-rate instruments will further need to match the period of each interest-rate reset, to eliminate spread risk.

Under cash-flow matching, there is no liquidity gap—at least in theory. Locking in terms and interest rate bases also locks in profit. For instance, a six-month, fixed-rate loan is funded with a six-month, fixed-rate deposit. This would eliminate both liquidity risk and interest-rate risk. In a customer-focused business it may not be possible to precisely match assets and liabilities, but from a macro-level it should be possible to match the profiles fairly closely, by netting—and matching—total exposure on both sides.

Is it desirable to run a matched book? Maybe not. In such a scenario the ALM book offers no view on the direction of interest rates. A part of the banking book is usually left unmatched, and it is this part that benefits (or loses out) if rates go as expected (or not).

Gap Management

We noted in the previous section the method of matching assets with liabilities. However, this is not always practical for a number of reasons, including the need to meet client demand and to maximise return on capital. More active ALM strategies are called for and gap management is one of them.

This term describes the practice of varying the gap between asset and liability in response to forecasts about interest rates and the shape of the yield curve. Simply put, this means increasing the gap when interest rates are likely to rise, and decreasing it when rates are likely to fall. The gap being managed here is the difference between floating-rate assets and liabilities. The gap also needs to be managed when either is fixed rate.

Gap management assumes that the ALM manager is correctly forecasting the direction of interest rates and the yield curve. An incorrect forecast can lead to a widening or

---

[2] Many bank assets, such as residential mortgages and credit-card loans, are repaid before their legal maturity date. Thus the size of the asset book is constantly amortising.

narrowing of the gap spread, and thus to losses. The ALM manager must choose the level of trade-off between risk and return.

Gap management also assumes that the profile of the banking book can be altered with relative ease. This is not always the case, however, and remains a problem despite the evolution of a liquid market in off-balance-sheet, interest-rate derivatives. Historically, changing the structure of the book has been difficult, as many loans cannot be liquidated instantly and fixed-rate assets and liabilities cannot be changed to floating-rate. Client relationships must also be observed and maintained—a key banking issue.

For these reasons, it is far more common for ALM managers to use off-balance-sheet products when dynamically managing the book (for example, forward rate agreements or FRAs to hedge gap exposure, or interest-rate swaps to alter an interest basis from fixed to floating, or vice-versa).

Securitisation

Securitisation is an important ALM tool for banks. A well-established procedure in the global debt-capital markets, securitisation spreads risk by re-packaging loans into pools and issuing new securities backed by the underlying loan pools. So a bank will sell assets, which generate cash-flows from the institution that owns the assets, to another company specifically set up to acquire them. The second company then issues notes backed by the cash-flows from the original assets.

The technique was first introduced as a means of funding in the 1970s by mortgage banks in the United States, and subsequently was applied to other assets such as credit-card payments and equipment-leasing receivables. The term 'securitisation' derives from the fact that the instruments used to obtain funds from investors come in the form of securities. The procedure incurs significant costs, including expenses for underwriting and credit-risk guarantees.

Securitisation forms part of ALM strategy to manage balance-sheet risk. A bank may securitise part of its balance sheet:

- if revenues received from assets remain roughly unchanged but the size of assets decreases, there will be an increase in the return on asset ratio;
- in instances where the level of capital required to support the balance sheet will be reduced, which again can lead to cost savings or allow the institution to allocate the capital to other, perhaps more profitable, business;
- to obtain cheaper funding: frequently the interest payable on asset-backed securities is considerably below the level receivable on the underlying loans. This creates a cash surplus for the originating entity.

The market for asset-backed securities (ABS) is estimated at US$1 trillion annually in investments worldwide, which actually represents a sharp decline from an estimated

FIGURE 2.7   Asset-backed securities stock

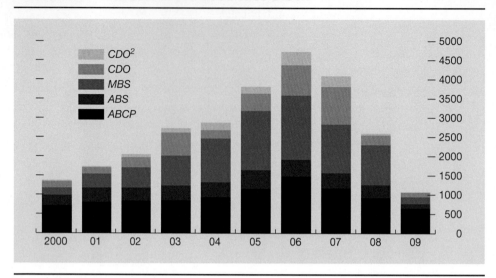

US$4 trillion before the global financial crisis. (See Figure 2.7.) Securitisation allows a bank certain benefits, including the following:

- **Access to alternative funding sources for other uses.** The fund may be at a lower cost and/or more reliable than the traditional forms of unsecured banking financing. As such, access to this source of funding enables a bank to grow its loan books at a faster pace. For example, Northern Rock, a former building society turned bank in the UK, has used securitisation to back its growing share of the UK residential mortgage market.
- **Reshaping of its asset portfolio.** Banks generally do not wish to be reliant on limited sources of funding, as that can be highly risky in economic downturns. Banks aim to optimise their funding between a mix of retail, interbank and wholesale sources. Securitisation has a key role to play in this mix.
- **Reduction in funding costs.** The securitisation process de-links the credit rating of the originating institution from the credit rating of the issued notes. Typically, most of the notes issued by the specially created company will be higher rated than the bonds issued directly by the originating bank.

Formulating a Capital Planning Policy

The importance of a strong capital planning process emerged as one of the key lessons of the global financial crisis, which was exacerbated by weaknesses in bank processes 'that were not sufficiently comprehensive, appropriately forward-looking or adequately formalised,' according to the BCBS.[3] Even without clear information about the prevalent market conditions, banks continued to pay dividends and repurchase commons shares even though capital could have been kept in house to protect them against future losses.

The BCBS says there are 'four fundamental components of a sound capital planning process'. These are:

- **Internal control and governance:** The capital planning process must include input from across the bank including, at the very least, experts from the business, risk, finance and treasury departments. It is key that there be a strong link between capital planning, budgeting and strategic planning. Without all this input, banks could end up with plans that do not reflect the strategy of individual business lines. One sound practice is to expose plans to external validation to ensure processes are strong and uniformly applied. The board of directors and one or more committees should review and approve once a year.
- **Capital policy and risk capture:** Capital policies should reference both capital and performance metrics that monitor the condition of the bank, including Common Equity Tier 1 ratio, as well as non-regulatory metrics that focus on returns including ROE, risk-adjusted return on capital (RAROC) and return on risk-adjusted capital (RORAC). Monitoring risk and its relationship to capital is not enough, however. Banks need to develop a formal escalation protocol for times when a risk limit or a trigger is hit.
- **Forward looking view:** Stress testing and scenario analysis are important components of capital planning. These are two techniques to arrive at a forward view of the capital base of a bank. Without this type of forward-looking view, a capital plan could be very vulnerable to, or inadequate for, market conditions.
- **Management framework for preserving capital:** Senior management and directors should rely on the capital planning process to arrive at their views of how vulnerable the bank is to changes in market or economic conditions. It is up to both management and directors to make sure that monitoring and escalation protocols, risk reporting and stress testing remain relevant. They are also responsible for knowing what capital actions are available for dealing with unexpected events.

ALCO Plan

The ALCO is particularly important for banks and financial institutions because it formulates the asset and liability management strategy that the bank follows. The strategy is instrumental in controlling the key risks that the bank faces. The concept of risk is not inherently a bad one. Risk-taking is very much a part of a bank's business activities and thus a

---

[3] Bank for International Settlements. 'A Sound Capital Planning Process: Fundamental Elements'. January 2014.

big part of ALM. Part of developing an ALCO plan is identifying the various risks that an institution faces and then determining the level of exposure that it might be comfortable with. Figure 2.8 shows what experts consider as the elements of a good risk management system. Note the place ALCO occupies in this chart.

FIGURE 2.8 Elements of a sound risk management system

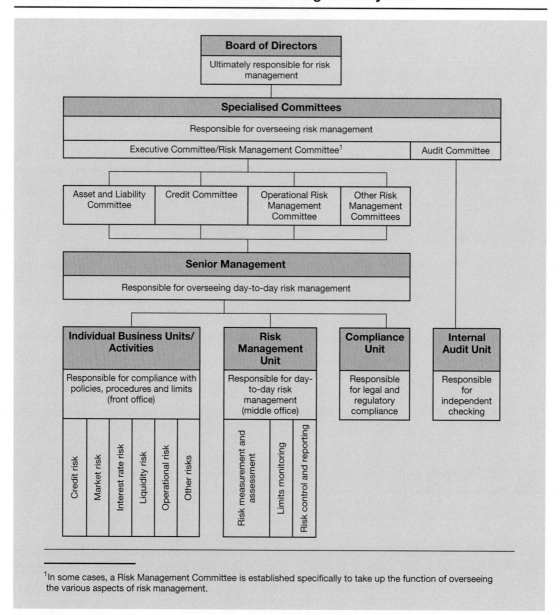

[1]In some cases, a Risk Management Committee is established specifically to take up the function of overseeing the various aspects of risk management.

Source: HKIB

Before delving further into what an ALCO plan entails, it is important to understand what the various categories of risk are. Other books in this series, including *Credit Risk Management* and *Treasury Markets and Operations* consider risks in greater detail. Here, we will briefly look at and define the most salient risk categories before moving on to other considerations necessary to develop an ALCO plan.

In its 'Supervisory Policy Manual', the HKMA makes clear what is expected of AIs in Hong Kong with regards to risks. Clause 1.1 on General Risk Management Controls states: 'Risk-taking is an integral part of banking business. Each AI has to find an appropriate balance between the level of risk it is willing to take and the level of return it desires to achieve.'

'An effective risk management system that is commensurate with the size and complexity of [each AI's] operations needs to be in place,' the policy manual goes on, 'to help ensure that the risks undertaken are well managed within the AI's risk appetite and that it achieves the intended results.'

What are these risks? The following are the inherent risks in banking that financial institutions must pay particular attention to:

- **Liquidity risk:** Ranging from customer demands for funds (withdrawals from chequing accounts, for example) to loan commitments, letters of credit, and derivatives.
- **Interest-rate risk:** A bank faces the risk that interest rates on its liabilities will climb, thereby reducing the profit it earns from interest on its assets.
- **Credit risk:** Each time a bank lends to a customer, it faces the risk of a default. If a payment is not made within a stipulated time, a loan is usually written off. Banks therefore need to maintain certain reserves to cover such losses.
- **Trading risk:** Consisting of price risk, interest-rate risk and foreign-exchange risk. A bank can earn huge profits by trading debt securities and derivatives. The risk of such trading can be measured by sophisticated statistical tools and financial models, but as the 2008 economic crises illustrated, none of these are fool-proof.
- **Operational risk:** This is the risk of destruction to a bank's offices, equipment, property and other items it needs in order to operate. Man-made attacks such as that on the World Trade Center in 2001, or natural disasters such as Hurricane Katrina in 2005, can cause collateral damage to the operations of banks and businesses in the stricken areas. Operational risk also arises from bad business practices.
- **Reputation risk:** Perceived or real financial weaknesses and fraudulent practices within a bank often lead to a flight of capital and a shortage of incoming funds.
- **Legal risk:** Banks need to contend with the risk of legal suits, unfavourable judgements and toothless contracts that may affect their operations unfavourably.
- **Strategic risk:** This refers to the risk that is inherent in profit-making strategies such as expansion of operations, mergers and acquisitions and divestiture of assets.

As we mentioned above, these are the most salient of risks. There are others, of course. It is important for professionals involved in developing the ALCO's plan to be intimately familiar with all of them and understand the conditions that can lead to risk events.

The committee makes its decisions based, in large part, on the ALCO package or ALCO pack. The ALCO pack is a package of reports that includes financial information related to the work of the ALCO. The package typically includes yield curve assumptions, net interest income projections and the economic value of equity assessments done in the normal course of business planning.

Sustainable Growth Model

For banking professionals, risk considerations are important but they are not the focus of their activity. Rather, risk considerations are an important part of developing a plan that puts the bank on a path towards growth, ideally sustainable growth. The ideas behind sustainable growth have gained considerable traction since the global financial crisis (GFC) of 2008. Hong Kong banks, which are generally conservative and well capitalised, by and large made it through the crisis with flying colours. Nevertheless, the crisis brought the importance of sustainable growth for both individual banks and entire banking systems into stark relief.

The crisis brought the idea of capital controls back into fashion. These controls include capital management techniques, including exchange controls, capital controls and prudential regulations.[4] The importance of sustainable growth has been highlighted time and again, and governments have worked towards this goal for decades. Regulators put in the first set of modern controls for banks in the aftermath of the Great Depression of 1930 and these controls held for about three decades after the Second World War.

Basking in the warm glow of post-war growth and facing pressure from financial interests around the world, regulators started to relax their watch in the 1980s. Around the same time, however, financial innovations led to the emergence of more varied and exotic financial instruments. The debate continues over whether all this financial innovation led to an almost constant stream of financial crises that started in 1997 with the Asian Financial Crisis and continued through to the GFC a decade later and arguably the European Debt Crisis of 2010. What is certain, however, is that regulators and individual institutions are much more aware of risk controls, the need to develop and follow a strong ALCO plan and the importance of ensuring sustainable growth models.

It is not entirely unfair to claim that most of the crises over the past few decades have, at least, a few roots in regulatory failures and the relative short sightedness of the private sector. The goal of much of the new regulation surrounding banks around the world, in particular the regulatory structures created by Basel II and Basel III, tackle these concerns. A key feature of the new regulations is to ensure the sustainable growth of financial institutions within a framework of sustainable growth of the broader economy.

---

[4] Epstein, Gerald. 'Capital management techniques to control financial risks and help achieve fair and sustainable growth.' In Watt, Andrew and Botsch, Andreas (eds) (2010) *After the crisis: towards a sustainable growth model*. Brussels: European Trade Union Institute.

To be truly successful, a sustainable growth model has to consider the bank's strategy, the institution's own return targets, capital adequacy, leverage and liquidity risk.

Putting in place a sustainable growth model for any financial institution is, perhaps, the key goal of an ALCO plan. The plan provides a general direction for the bank. It is up to other departments to implement the specific bank policies that will ensure the ALCO's direction is followed.

The idea that the bank's overall strategy has to follow a sustainable growth model is not entirely new. Sustainable growth has been a goal for financial institutions since time immemorial. What the ALCO plan can do is incorporate the latest thinking and regulatory requirements and ensure the bank's overall strategy fits. Before the GFC, most bank regulation was very narrow in its focus and did not look at the systemic linkages within the financial system that could create chain effects in one or more areas of risks. Even years after the crash, the links within the financial sector are often ignored by industry specific regulation but left up to public policy. This is changing somewhat but it is something for the ALCO and the broader financial institution it serves. Even when there is no regulation, the risk control recommendations of the ALCO can help ensure that banks follow sustainable growth patterns. At times, this might mean avoiding business areas that are perfectly allowed by regulators but might be outside the bank's own sustainable strategy for growth.[5]

No sustainable growth plan is complete without return targets. Banks and financial institutions are, after all, for-profit institutions with shareholders who expect returns on their equity. As part of its plan, the ALCO should consider what the appropriate return targets are for the institution and ensure that those returns are achievable without jeopardising the bank's capital, liquidity or leverage position.

Not to be confused with liquidity, the bank's capital position at the end of each day is a key indicator of performance and one that regulators may carefully scrutinise. The capital adequacy ratio (CAR) is a calculation of the bank's capital base to its risk-weighted assets and it is used to determine a bank's position as it relates to its exposure to credit risk, market risk and operational risk. In Hong Kong, the Banking Ordinance requires locally incorporated AIs to maintain a minimum CAR of 8% but that can be increased to as much as 16%. The HKMA assigns each bank a minimum ratio based on its specific position while the Banking (Capital) Rules of the HKMA outline how banks should calculate their individual CAR.

Putting in place policies to deal with liquidity risk is another important consideration for the ALCO and its plan for the bank. No growth plan will be sustainable for long if it doesn't take liquidity considerations into account. For financial institutions in Hong Kong, and in just about every other jurisdiction that follows the Basel principles, failure to meet liquidity targets can have serious implications not only for the bottom line of a bank but also for its regulatory standing. Managing liquidity requires a thorough understanding of a bank's operations and needs on a day-to-day basis as well as careful

---

[5] Sriram, M.S., Chaturvedi, Vaibhav and Neti, Annapurna (2012) 'Too big to fail versus too small to be counted' in *BIS Papers No 62*. Bank for International Settlements: www.bis.org.

consideration of the daily liabilities that a bank has to meet. A bank with a large network of branches may, for example, tap into retail deposits to meet its liquidity requirements while banks that are more focused on wholesale business may find it more practical and economic to borrow from the market to obtain short-term liquidity.

The bank's strategy to fund its liquidity needs should match its footprint and the scope of its activities. The ALCO should generally avoid concentrations of risk, such as relying too much on a single lender or one provider of liquidity. It should also consider that some sources of liquidity fluctuate more than others. Cash deposits may, for example, drop significantly during slow periods, or holidays, or in times of economic stress.[6]

As with most other aspects of managing the assets and liabilities of a bank, no one area is truly independent of the others. Managing liquidity is one key goal of the ALCO plan but so is managing the bank's leverage position. The amount of leverage both on and off balance sheet, has a direct impact on the amount of liquidity that a bank might need on any given day.

Medium and Long-Term ALM Strategy

Short-term goals, such as meeting daily liquidity requirements, are important parts of the bank's ALM strategy but they are not enough, on their own. An effective ALCO plan also takes into consideration both medium and long-term strategies. The nature of modern banks is such that ALCOs have to look several years into the future as they prepare their plans. Interest rates, for example are subject to change, as are foreign exchange rates, inflation and even the liquidity and capital requirements that a bank or other financial institution may have to adhere to.

Consider a fictitious bank that borrows US$100 million at 3% for one year but then lends that same amount to a borrower at a rate of 3.20% for five years with interest compounded annually to maturity. On the face of it, the transaction looks profitable as the bank is earning 20 basis points, but a more careful look suggests there are plenty of risks. A key risk is repricing. The bank will have to find new financing for the loan at the end of the year because it has four years to go. Suppose that at the end of Year 1 the bank can only find financing at 6%. Should this happen the bank would be in trouble as it is now earning 3.20% on funds for which it is paying 6%. Using a market-value accounting method, the transaction could end up costing the bank more than US$10 million. A key goal of the ALCO plan is avoiding these types of mismatches.

---

[6]The HKMA considers liquidity risk management at length in its 'Supervisory Policy Manual'. More information can be found online. Liquidity Risk Management, LM-1 of July 29, 2016. http://www.hkma.gov.hk/media/eng/doc/key-functions/banking-stability/supervisory-policy-manual/LM-1.pdf.

And this loss does not even take into consideration other risks like credit default. Consider for a moment that interest rates fall substantially and, at the end of the year, the bank ends up refinancing the same loan at 1%. Suddenly, the risk of credit default rises as the customer finds itself paying significantly more than the going rate for the funds.

Another consideration, one that extends to both scenarios, is liquidity. The ALCO plan has to consider how the bank's operations will affect its liquidity in the medium and long term. The bank should know where its liquidity will come from at all times. Banks that earn large mark-to-market profits can go bankrupt if they lack adequate cash flow.

Ultimately, ALCO's plan to manage asset and liabilities is a strategic decision-making tool. The ALCO plan is not there to eliminate or minimise risk but to develop strategies to optimise financial results. One way to look at this is to follow the definition of modern ALM that the Society of Actuaries' Task Force on ALM Principles has developed: 'ALM is the ongoing process of formulating, implementing, monitoring and revising strategies related to assets and liabilities to achieve the financial objectives for a given set of risk tolerances and constraints.'

Table 2.1 outlines the purpose and scope of ALCO as set by the Bank of England.

TABLE 2.1 The purpose and scope of ALCO set by the Bank of England

Purpose of ALCO	• to ensure that individual business lines are aligned in terms of the firm's overall objectives and proactively controlled, with regard to the prudential risks under the ALM's control (liquidity, and funding risk and interest-rate risk in the banking book); • to ensure that all ALM risks remain within the risk appetite set by the governing body; and • to evaluate and assess the impact of other potential drivers of earnings volatility, such as competitive pressures or non-interest rate related changes to market conditions.

Scope of ALCO	1. Asset and liability impacts of current operating plans, and market update;
	2. Liquidity and funding risk;
	3. Interest rate risk in the banking book (IRRBB) and other drivers of net interest income sensitivity
	  - non-traded market interest rate risk in the banking book including market index bases risks;
	  - structural non-discretionary interest rate risk in the banking book;
	  - other potential non-interest rate drivers of income volatility;
	4. Funds transfer pricing mechanism;
	5. Structural foreign exchange risk;
	6. Liquidity stress testing;
	7. Contingency funding plans.

Source: http://www.bankofengland.co.uk/publications/Documents/other/pra/policy/2013/assetliabilitymgmtlss1-13.pdf

Summary

- The Asset and Liability Management Committee or ALCO is responsible for setting and implementing Asset and Liability Management (ALM) policy. The ALCO meets regularly to deliberate on reports by the ALM or Treasury desks on interest income, areas experiencing income fluctuations, and short-term income projections.
- A bank's strategy for holding liquid assets should take into account the type and quality of the assets, as well as the amount. The most liquid asset is cash, followed by securities.
- In building its securities portfolio, a bank should consider secondary market liquidity, as well as strategies such as the ladder and split-maturity approaches. A bank's loan portfolio is an illiquid asset and carries significant risk. It must be monitored and its composition broken down by loan relationship and size, and by the bank's major lines of business.
- A deposit is a liability for a bank, but also a critical source of finance for the bank's lending activities. Customer deposits, securitisation, corporate loans and structured deposits are among the most prominent liabilities.
- Liquidity risk arises from normal banking operations, i.e. irrespective of the type of funding gap. Liquidity risk in itself generates interest-rate risk, due to the uncertainty of future interest rates.
- A bank should weigh the costs of each type of funding against the risks. A risk of withdrawal is associated with liabilities, and a risk of loss inherent in interest-rate changes.
- Matching assets with liabilities is not always practical for a bank. A more active ALM strategy is gap management, which is the practice of varying the gap between asset and liability in response to forecasts about interest rates and the shape of the yield curve.
- Securitisation spreads risk by re-packaging loans into pools and issuing new securities backed by the underlying loan pools.

Key Terms

Asset and Liability Management (ALM)
Asset and Liability Management
    Committee (ALCO)
Duration gap
Gap management
Hedging
Hong Kong Interbank Offered Rate
    (HIBOR)
Interest-rate gap
Ladder approach

London Interbank Offered Rate (LIBOR)
Matched-book approach
Maturity gap
Primary underwriting activities
Secondary market liquidity
Securities portfolio
Securitisation
Split-maturity approaches
Yield-curve strategies

Review Questions

1. What is the function of the Asset and Management Liability Committee (ALCO) and how do the various ALM desk reports facilitate the committee in carrying out its role?
2. How do interest-rate changes affect liability management?
3. Describe the typical composition of a bank's loan portfolio and explain why the composition is critical in loan portfolio management.
4. Describe and evaluate some of the well-known techniques to manage liquidity risk.

Further Reading

Choudhry, Moorad (2007) *Bank Asset and Liability Management: Strategy, Trading, Analysis*. Singapore: John Wiley & Sons (Asia) Pte Ltd.

Comptroller of the Currency: Administrator of National Banks. 'Loan Portfolio Management' in *Comptroller's Handbook*. 26 April 2010. http://www.occ.treas.gov/handbook/lpm.pdf.

Hong Kong Monetary Authority. http://www.info.gov.hk/hkma/.

_____. *The Composite Interest Rate of Hong Kong – A New Data Series*. 12 April 2010. http://www.info.gov.hk/hkma/eng/research/RM26-2005.pdf.

3

Managing Bank Assets and Liabilities

Learning outcomes

After studying this chapter, you should be able to:

1 Explain in broad terms how banks manage their assets and ensure they have sufficient liquidity to operate securely.

2 Describe the various types of activities involved in developing strong loan and investment portfolios.

3 Explain how banks manage their liabilities, including the various measures banks can take to ensure safe and effective liability management and access funds.

Introduction

The assets that modern banks hold have grown more complex than ever before, but the traditional business of lending is still very much key. Traditional wholesale and retail loans still represent the largest asset category for most banks.

Managing Bank Assets

Modern banks have to manage larger and more complicated asset portfolios in more heavily regulated environments than ever before. Banks in Hong Kong often hold multiple classes of assets including cash deposits, bonds, securities, loans, mortgages and a range of derivatives. To add complications to the mix, banks often hold assets in any of dozens of currencies. At the heart of it all is the largest asset category in the balance sheet of most banks: conventional lending. This lending is made up of loans to retail and wholesale loans.

Managing all these assets profitably over many years, and in varied economic conditions often spanning multiple markets, requires a carefully considered set of strategies. This is particularly true for a bank's more liquid assets. The strategies should cover both the type and quality of the assets that the bank is willing to hold as well as the quantity, often as a percentage of the bank's total assets.

Liquidity Management—Assets

The most liquid asset is cash. The bank is required by law to hold a certain amount of cash—or cash-like bonds—as reserves and most banks in Hong Kong keep excess reserves at hand. A bank must maintain cash or highly liquid assets to meet transactional needs as well as a growing set of regulatory requirements driven by local regulators and standards such as the Basel accords that are arrived at through transnational agreement. Beyond that, however, cash cannot be allowed to sit idle without incurring opportunity costs.

To determine the types and amounts to hold as liquid assets, the bank should consider a wide-ranging series of factors including:

- the daily cash requirements of the bank to meet client needs;
- regulatory requirements that set out how much cash banks should hold in reserve;
- depth and liquidity of the market, which can determine, for example, how swiftly the debt securities can be sold and at what price;
- in the case of securities, the banks should consider what percentage of a particular issue the bank holds as well as the credit ratings of the securities held;
- currency of denomination of the securities held;
- expected maturity date, taking into account the possibility of early redemption or disposal;

- probability of using the securities as collateral to borrow funds in the open market or from the central bank or monetary authority. In Hong Kong, Exchange Fund bills and Notes can be sold or pledged easily; they are eligible for rediscount at the Discount Window operated by the Hong Kong Monetary Authority if an authorised institution has a shortfall in its clearing balance. As such, several authorised institutions hold them for liquidity.

The Loan Portfolio

Loans and deposits make up the traditional banking activity recorded in the banking book. A loan portfolio is a major asset for a bank, and its largest source of revenue. It is listed as such on a bank's balance sheet. The value of a portfolio depends on the interest earned on the loans, and the creditworthiness of each loan, i.e. the probability of payment of the loan interest and principal.

But the greatest source of income for the bank is also its greatest source of worry. Lending makes a bank vulnerable to risks, including defaulting borrowers and volatile interest rates, flawed credit appraisals and a feeble economy.

Loan Portfolio Management

Elsewhere in this series we have discussed a bank's exposure to credit: how each time it lends, it faces the risk of a default, and how prudent banks can manage credit risk in a variety of ways. For example, they can: focus on loans to customers, with whom they have a transaction history; require collateral, thereby prompting borrowers to repay as quickly as possible; and analyse a borrower's creditworthiness, particularly if the applicant is not a bank customer.

The inherent risks in lending are monitored and controlled through Loan Portfolio Management (LPM). A booklet by the Comptroller of the Currency Administrator of National Banks of the US calls the LPM process a primary supervisory activity. The handbook notes that, for a long time, loan portfolio management focused on prudently approving loans and carefully monitoring loan performance. The booklet suggests bankers review not only the risks posed by each credit, but also how the risks of individual loans and portfolios are interrelated.

Composition of a Loan Portfolio

As mentioned earlier, a bank's loan portfolio is possibly its best-earning asset. The downside? A loan portfolio is an illiquid asset and carries significant risk. To manage that risk, a bank must monitor and manage its loan portfolio constantly. Reports on the portfolio composition should be constant and readily available. The total portfolio should be broken down by loan relationship and size, and by the bank's major lines of business. The number of loans, the loan relationships and the total balances outstanding should also be identified for each section based on size.

Banks and financial institutions divide loans into two categories: secured and unsecured. In a secured loan, the borrower offers some asset (a house, perhaps) as collateral. In an unsecured loan, as the name suggests, no asset is offered.

- **Secured loans.** Among the most common secured loans are those for housing, cars and consumer durables. A mortgage or loan to buy housing is an almost ubiquitous type of debt instrument. For the bank the security is in the form of a lien on the title to the house until the mortgage is fully paid. (A lien is the legal right to take and hold or sell the property of a debtor as security or payment for a debt or duty.) For car loans, a bank can lend directly to a customer, or indirectly through a car dealer. The tenure of a car loan is shorter than that for a home loan, and is often equivalent to the 'good years' of a vehicle's life, especially if the car is pledged as security.
- **Unsecured loans.** Banks offer loans without collateral in various ways. The interest charged for such loans varies depending on the debtor and creditor, and the law of the land. The types of unsecured loans include the following:
  - o *Credit card payments.* A customer can buy an item, without cash, by ringing it up on a credit card provided by a bank. The latter makes money on late-payment fees and charges.
  - o *Personal loans.* Interest rates are usually higher for a personal loan given without assets as security. If a personal loan is secured, terms of repayment are usually more flexible.
  - o *Bank overdrafts or lines of credit.* Simply a revolving loan, a bank overdraft makes credit available for borrowing and charges interest only on the daily overdraft (debit) balance. An overdraft is also a demand loan, and the outstanding amount can be 'called' at any time by the lender. A bank overdraft is known in US practice as a line of credit or credit line.

Let us now examine loans for business. Companies need working capital to finance expansion and acquisition. They can obtain funds through corporate bonds or debt financing, or through bank loans and lines of credit.

The corporate borrower must furnish the bank with suitable financial details and apply for the loan. If approved, the company is given a line of credit, which is then structured based on the borrower's requirement and the bank's facilities. Banks require a guarantee or collateral from the corporate borrower, although each institution has its own terms. The security for corporate loans, as for individual loans, takes the form of a lien on the collateral, to be exacted only in the case of default.

There are many types of corporate loans, and the importance of each depends upon geographical location and the specific industry. Some forms of corporate loans include:

- **Real estate financing.** This is a traditional activity for financial institutions such as banks and savings-and-loan associations that are offering corporate loans for land and property development, or as bridging loans. For banks, real-estate financing carries the same types of risk as do other financing activities, and therefore requires similar management of assets, and investment yield.

- **Performance bonds and guarantees.** Companies sometimes need these to demonstrate their creditworthiness when they want to participate in a contract or enter into a transaction with another company. A bank issues a performance bond to one party as a guarantee against the other party failing to meet its contractual obligations. A bank guarantee works in much the same way. The bank guarantees that the liabilities being incurred by the corporation will be met. In the event the company defaults, the debt will be covered by the bank.
- **Debt capital market products.** These include syndicated loans, floating- and variable-rate notes, fixed-rate bonds and commercial paper. Banks offer these products for medium and long-term financing. In a syndicated loan, a group of banks lends to a corporate borrower. The loan's interest rate is usually linked to a variable rate index such as LIBOR (London Interbank Offered Rate) or the bank's rates on Certificates of Deposit.

The Investment Portfolio

After cash, securities comprise the most liquid portion of a bank's assets. Banks are active in both the primary and secondary markets, and when building their securities portfolios should take the following issues into account.

- **Primary underwriting activities.** The primary market is the market for issue of new securities. Investment banks raise funds by selling equity and debt-capital securities to investors on behalf of companies and governments. As underwriters of the issue, the banks take on the risk of distributing the securities, but make their money on the difference between the price they pay to the issuer for the securities, and the price they get when they sell the securities to investors and/or brokers.
- **Secondary market liquidity.** After the initial offer in the primary market, shares are traded in the secondary market. The latter is where most securities activity occurs. A bank should hold securities with secondary market liquidity. In other words, they can be sold quickly, during trading hours, with a minimum loss of value and price change.
- **Maturity strategies.** The bank can devise and employ maturity strategies such as:
  i. **The ladder approach.** Also known as the spaced-maturity approach, this entails investing funds equally across securities of several maturity intervals within a bank's investment horizon. This easily managed technique reduces income fluctuation and increases the opportunity to benefit from cash rollover.
  ii. **Split-maturity approaches.** These include the following:
     - The *barbell approach* invests funds in a combination of short-term and long-term securities, and a small amount of funds in intermediate-term

securities. The investment strategy is useful to meet short-term liquidity needs.

- The *front-end loaded approach* invests mainly in short-term securities, thereby stressing liquidity needs. The emphasis on short-term securities guards against huge financial losses due to sudden hikes in interest rates.

- The *back-end loaded approach* invests mainly in long-term securities, thereby stressing return. The strategy makes the securities portfolio a source of income; it helps to maximise income from securities when interest rates fall. Like the front-end loaded approach, it does not invest in intermediate securities.

- **Yield-curve strategies.** Yield-curve strategies refer to the adjustment of a bank's securities portfolio with expected changes in interest rates. A yield curve represents the maturity of securities and their yields to maturity at a specific point of time. A security positioned above the curve indicates a 'buy' decision, while a security below indicates a 'sell'. A yield curve's shape and level gives information about managing the securities portfolio:

  i. When a steeply rising yield curve is at a lower level, a bank can shift investment in longer-term securities to shorter-term securities. The bank can thereby earn the expected future high yields through a repeated rollover of short-term securities and avoid capital losses from longer-term securities.

  ii. On the other hand, when a downward-sloped yield curve is at a higher level, a bank should put more funds in longer-term securities than in short-term. An expected fall in interest rates will mean capital gains in longer-term securities.

    A bank can also try for higher yields through re-investment and selling of securities by *'riding' the yield curve*. When a yield curve is upward-sloping and interest-rate stability is likely in the near future, the bank can: buy securities with maturities longer than the investment horizon; sell the longer-term securities when they reach the investment horizon in order to obtain capital gains due to the fall in yields as they approach their maturities; and re-invest the proceeds in longer-term securities with higher yields.

- **Duration management.** Another strategy to oversee a securities portfolio is duration management. What is 'duration'? It is a weighted average time-to-maturity on all cash flows associated with an asset or a liability. The formula for duration is given below.

$$\text{Duration} = \frac{\begin{array}{c}\text{Summation of present values of cash flows}\\ \text{at the end of period } t \text{ multiplied by } t\end{array}}{\text{Summation of present values of all cash flows}}$$

The duration number is a complicated calculation involving present value, yield, coupon, final maturity and call features. The indicator, however, is a standard data point provided in the presentation of comprehensive bond and bond mutual fund information. It is worth pointing out that a bond's investment value is affected by credit risk and interest-rate risk, and the duration indicator addresses the latter. Short-term, intermediate-term and long-term bond funds will have different durations.

Below are some useful points to note in managing duration:

- Duration measures average time required to recover the funds invested.
- The weights are in fact the present values of each cash-flow, relative to the present value of all cash-flows, i.e. market price.
- Duration increases when maturity increases, but at a diminishing rate. It is easy to understand that duration increases as maturity increases because of a longer time period needed to generate the cash-flows to recover the funds. When maturity increases, the discount rates for cash-flows in the farther future will be higher than those of the nearer future. This is why duration increases with maturity at a reducing rate.
- Duration decreases when yield to maturity increases. The higher the yield is to maturity, the faster the initial funds are recovered.
- Duration decreases when coupon rate increases. The larger the coupon payment, the faster the initial funds are recovered.
- Duration is also a measure of the interest sensitivity of the market price of an asset or a liability. A larger duration implies that the market price of an asset or a liability is more sensitive to a change in interest rate.

Managing Bank Liabilities

What are a bank's liabilities? Simply, they are the funds owed by a bank. In a balance sheet they are usually represented on the right hand side, with the assets on the left hand. A deposit placed in a bank is an asset for the customer, but a liability for the bank, because the latter must not only pay back the deposit, possibly on demand, but also may have to pay interest on it.

Liquidity Management—Liabilities

For the purposes of this section, we will look briefly at management of liquid liabilities. The first step for a bank, of course, is to choose its portfolio of liabilities carefully in order to maintain diversified and stable sources of funding. It must ascertain the appropriate mix of liabilities, and then build strong and lasting relationships with key fund providers.

To help manage the risks of deposit withdrawals and of the costs of liabilities, a bank could adopt the following measures:

- **Avoid undue concentration.** A bank should avoid undue focus on any particular type of liability. To assess the degree of liability concentration, the bank should consider the following aspects:
  i. Maturity profile and credit-sensitivity of the liability

    ii.   Mix of secured and unsecured funding

    iii. Extent of reliance on a single liability provider or a related group of liability providers, and on particular instruments or products and intragroup funding

    iv. Geographic location, industry or economic sector of liability providers.

- **Establish proportion of 'core' deposits.** Local banks with extensive branch networks tend to have more stable funding sources as retail deposits are usually less vulnerable to small interest-rate changes than are wholesale or large institutional deposits. When assessing the stability of liabilities, banks should also establish the approximate percentage of 'core' deposits.

- **Seek alternative funding sources.** Wholesale banks or foreign banks with a limited number of branches (and hence lacking a strong retail deposit base) need to seek alternative funding sources. Borrowing from the interbank market is one way, but depends on a number of factors, including the size and turnover of the local market and credit limits imposed by counterparties.

- **Estimate borrowing capacity in normal times.** Banks can regularly 'test their name' in the market to assess their borrowing capacity even if they have no immediate need for funds.

- **Establish standby credit lines.** Banks may also build and monitor their relationships with their main providers of funds. Standby credit lines may be arranged, with a keen eye open for associated risks, such as calls for early repayment of drawings, triggered by defaults or breaches of material adverse change clauses.

- **Develop ability to sell assets.** Another way to access other wholesale markets for funding is to sell assets in the market. Some of the ways to obtain additional liquidity under adverse circumstances include the following:

    i.   Add a sale clause in loan documentation

    ii. Use securitisation structures

    iii. Explore arrangements under repurchase agreements.

Sources of Funds

Nonetheless, as this section shows, deposits are a critical source of funds for the bank's lending activities. The most prominent liabilities for most banks are the following:

- **Customer deposits** are a key source of funds for a bank, particularly one with an extensive branch network. In such a scenario, a bank has a reasonably stable retail deposit base, and these deposits are less sensitive to small changes in interest rates than are wholesale or institutional large deposits. Retail customers deposit money in a bank for safekeeping and returns.

- **Transaction deposits** (current accounts or chequing accounts) are the most common form of customer deposits. Also known as demand deposits because they can be 'called' at any time, transaction deposits are sometimes listed separate from customer deposits in the balance sheet. They make up a large part of the M1 money supply.

- **Savings account deposits** are not as readily accessible to a customer as deposits in a chequing account, but they pay out interest to a customer. For the customer, this means access to liquidity and getting a monetary return in the bargain.
- **Money-market deposits** offer a higher rate of interest and require a relatively short notice for withdrawal. In the US, money-market deposits are considered instant-access deposits but subject to federal regulations.
- **Fixed or time deposits** are so called because the funds are locked in with the bank for a specified term. The money can be either withdrawn or rolled over when the term ends. Interest rates on a time deposit generally are higher the longer the 'fixed' period.

Interbank Borrowing

Wholesale banks or foreign banks with a limited branch network, and therefore without a stable retail deposit base, seek alternative access to funding—the interbank market, for example. The interbank market is the financial system and trading of currencies among banks and financial institutions, excluding retail investors and smaller trading parties.

A bank can use the interbank market to transfer funds and currency, and to manage liquidity. When it needs to replenish short-term cash reserves, the bank may borrow from an interbank market at interest rates set for that particular market. For example, debtors and creditors dealing in Asian economies could trade in Hong Kong dollars at the Hong Kong Interbank Offer Rate or HIBOR. Other banks may borrow money in the London interbank market at the London Interbank Offer Rate or LIBOR. The latter is used widely to benchmark short-term interest rates. The exact LIBOR and HIBOR rate fixing mechanism are set to be modified in future once the global LIBOR review initiative is being finalised.[1]

Another increasingly popular interest rate benchmark in Hong Kong is the CNH-HIBOR fixing which was launched in 2013.[2] Hong Kong is now the world's largest offshore RMB centre and such role will increase with the Belt and Road Initiative and the internationalisation of RMB after the Chinese currency became a Special Drawing Right (SDR) currency in October 2016.

A bank's capacity to borrow from the interbank market depends on several factors, including the size and turnover of the local market, credit limits imposed by counterparties and the individual institution's share of the market.

Securities

Securities are broadly divided into debt and equity. The debt component consists of bank-notes, bonds and debentures, and the equity consists mainly of stock which is the equity

---

[1]http://www.fsb.org/wp-content/uploads/Second-Review-of-the-Implementation-of-IOSCO%E2%80%99s-Principles-for-Financial-Benchmarks-by-Administrators-of-EURIBOR-LIBOR-and-TIBOR.pdf.

[2]https://www.tma.org.hk/en_newsevents_n1.aspx?NewsId=241.

capital required to absorb loss and provide for future investment needs. Such loss may include impairment of assets or off-balance-sheet transactions considered 'contingent liabilities' of a bank. They refer to a future exposure contracted in the present time. In most cases, these items do not generate cash inflow or outflow at inception, unlike a cash transaction, but represent future exposure. Under the risk-based capital guidelines approved by most countries' regulators, banks are required to hold a portion of equity capital in reserve to meet contingent obligations in off-balance-sheet items.

Structured Deposits

Another liability for a bank is a structured deposit. This is a mix of a deposit and an investment product, and the bank as issuer is obliged to repay the principal in full when the structured deposit matures, as well as any returns on the deposit and investment products.

Although structured deposits usually offer returns higher than those offered on fixed deposits, the actual returns are based on the performance of the financial instruments underlying the investment product. These instruments could be equities, fixed-income instruments, foreign exchange, or a collection of these. The amount payable will depend on their market value, which cannot be pre-determined.

If the underlying instrument performs badly, an investor could get little or no return on the investment product. Moreover, an early redemption could mean the investor loses a chunk of the principal invested. For the bank, the structured deposit is a liability, even when it is doing badly.

Interest-Rate Change

Net interest spread is the percentage point difference between the interest rate a bank earns on its assets and the interest rate it pays on its liabilities (e.g. bank deposits). Because it is a good indicator of the profitability of an institution's interest income, net income spread is a useful benchmark in ALM.

Interest-rate changes tend to have an impact on a bank's liability costs. Chequing accounts, which pay little or no interest, may be barely affected, short-term and floating-rate loans would be considerably affected. In general, high interest rates mean higher earnings for banks; lower interest rates mean lower earnings. A bank with a large number of fixed-rate loans in its portfolio would lose out with high interest rates, however, as it would earn less than it could.

In rare instances, interest rates for long-term funds will be lower than those for short-term deposits. An inverted yield curve occurs, and is considered an indicator of an uncertain economic situation ahead. In recessionary times, some central banks have chosen to adopt the zero interest rate policy (ZIRP) to help the economy to recover.

Summary

- Managing assets profitably requires a careful set of strategies that take into account both the quality and quantity of assets that a bank holds.
- To determine the types and amounts of liquid assets to hold banks should consider their daily cash requirements, regulatory requirements, depth and liquidity of the market, how much of a particular issue the bank holds (in the case of securities), credit ratings, currency of denomination, maturity dates and the possibility of early redemption and the possibility of using securities as collateral to borrow other funds.
- Loan portfolios are, traditionally, the single largest asset category in the balance sheets of most banks.
- Loan Portfolio Management is used to monitor and control the risks associated with lending. Banks should take into consideration both the risks associated with individual loans and with entire loan portfolios.
- Banks provide both secured and unsecured loans. Secured loans include loans for housing, cars and consumer durables. Perhaps the most common of such loans are mortgages, secured against the title of a home. Unsecured loans are not backed by any specific collateral and include such products as credit card payments, personal loans, bank overdrafts and lines of credit.
- Banks also provide a range of loan facilities to businesses. The importance of these facilities depends on the type of bank and its geographic location. These corporate loans include real estate financing, performance bonds and guarantees and debt capital market products.
- Securities make up most of the assets of a bank after cash and banks tend to be active in both primary and secondary markets for securities. They are involved in primary market underwriting for new security issues and in the secondary market to trade and hold shares for their own book and others.
- Banks employ a number of maturity strategies to manage their investments. These strategies include a ladder approach, investing across several maturity intervals, and split-maturity approaches, such as a barbell, front-end loaded and back-end loaded approaches.
- Banks use yield-curve strategies to adjust portfolios of securities to changes in interest rates. When a steep upward curve is at a lower level than the yield of a particular security a bank can shift investment to shorter-term securities but when a downward curve is at a higher level banks can shift over to longer-term securities. Banks can also try to 'ride' the yield curve by re-investing and selling securities.
- Using duration management banks can use a weighted average time to maturity on cash flows. The duration number is calculated using present value, yield, coupon, final maturity and call features. Duration measures the average time that might be required to recover the funds invested.

- Banks must also carefully manage their bank liabilities to avoid undue concentration, establish an adequate proportion of core deposits, seek alternative funding sources, estimate borrowing capacity, establish standby credit lines and develop an ability to sell assets.
- Deposits are a critical source of funds for a bank's lending activities.
- Banks often rely on the interbank market as an alternative source of funds, to transfer funds and currency and manage their daily liquidity.
- Securities can be either debt or equity.
- Structured deposits are both a deposit and an investment product, with the bank obliged to repay the principal in full when the structured deposit matures.
- The net interest spread is the percentage point difference between the interest rate a bank earns on its assets and the rate it pays on its liabilities. Changes in interest rates affect the spread, while managing the spread effectively is a key activity for banks.

Key Terms

Assets
Back-end loaded approach
Barbell approach
Contingent liabilities
Credit card payments
Credit lines
Currency
Customer deposits
Deposits
Discount window
Duration management
Exchange fund
Fixed deposits
Front-end loaded approach
Interbank market
Interest rates
Ladder approach
Liabilities
Liquid assets
Liquid liabilities
Liquidity
Loan portfolio

Loan portfolio management
Market liquidity
Maturity
Money market deposits
Mortgages
Primary underwriting
Reserve requirement ratio
'Riding' the yield curve
Savings account deposits
Secondary underwriting
Secured loans
Split-maturity
Spreads
Structured deposits
Time deposits
Transaction deposits
Underwriting
Unsecured loans
Yield curve
Yield-curve strategies
Zero Interest Rate Policy (ZIRP)

Review Questions

1. Why do banks consider loans to be assets? What other assets do banks typically hold? How do they manage these assets?
2. What is duration management? How do banks use it to manage their liquid assets?
3. What are some sources of funds that banks can access to manage their liabilities?
4. Explain interbank networks and how banks can use them to manage their liquidity.

Further Reading

Choudhry, Moorad (2007) *Bank Asset and Liability Management: Strategy, Trading, Analysis*. Singapore: John Wiley & Sons (Asia) Pte Ltd.

Comptroller of the Currency: Administrator of National Banks. 'Loan Portfolio Management' in *Comptroller's Handbook*. 26 April 2010. http://www.occ.treas.gov/handbook/lpm.pdf.

Hong Kong Monetary Authority. http://www.info.gov.hk/hkma/.

_____. *The Composite Interest Rate of Hong Kong – A New Data Series*. 12 April 2010. http://www.info.gov.hk/hkma/eng/research/RM26-2005.pdf.

PART 2

MANAGING LIQUIDITY RISK AND INTEREST RATE RISK

4

Liquidity Management

After studying this chapter, you should be able to:

1 Define key concepts used in measuring liquidity risk including the liquidity coverage ratio, the net stable funding ratio and the BCBS principles to manage liquidity risk.

2 Describe the funding needs of banks, including loan and deposit trend forecasting, meeting liquidity gaps and liquidity planning.

3 Explain the role of stress testing in managing liquidity.

Introduction

Liquidity is key to the operations of banks and other financial institutions, and managing liquidity risk is a very important function that is often overlooked. At times, the need for liquidity can override profitability or the choice of products that a bank handles. The liquidity resources of a bank are important factors in determining the credit-worthiness of the institution itself as well as the rating accorded to it by agencies like Moody's, Standard & Poor's or Fitch Ratings. At the end of the day, liquidity and solvency are inter-related. Without adequate liquidity, banks may not be able to meet their obligations, even if they have a positive balance sheet.

Effective liquidity management is an intrinsic part of effective bank asset and liability management (BALM). In fact, it is almost impossible to properly manage the latter without effectively managing the former. Liquidity risk is, at the end of the day, one of the key risks that banks have to consider as part of their operations. Liquidity risk comes into play in a broad range of operational areas and can be affected by legal and tax events or regulatory requirements, to name just two examples. At its very core, liquidity risk is the risk that a bank or other authorised institution (AI) may be unable to meet its obligations as they fall due. This inability to meet obligations could be caused by a variety of factors including an AI's ability to liquidate assets or access short-term funding through discount windows or interbank facilities. Problems can also be caused by problems of liquidity in the broader market at times of crisis.[1] At times of dropping interest rates or slowing economic growth, liquidity risk generally rises and drops as economic recovery kicks in and interest rates start to go up, to mention but one overly simplified example. (See Lehman Brothers case study in Chapter 7.)

This chapter considers the definition and measures of liquidity, including the principles on liquidity management used by the Basel Committee on Banking Supervision (BCBS), the liquidity coverage ratio and the net stable funding ratio. A second section then looks at how banks and financial institutions determine their funding needs and this is followed by a look at how stress tests are implemented and the role they play in managing liquidity.

It is key for banking professionals to understand how individual banks and other AIs manage their liquidity. It is also key for them to have a solid grasp of the factors that go into determining what an adequate level of liquidity is, and the tools that banks and regulators use to ensure that banks have enough liquidity on hand at all times. These tools have become increasingly sophisticated over the decades, as both practitioners and regulators learn painful lessons from times of crisis, bank runs and failures that are, if not frequent, far too common.

---

[1] For a much longer discussion of the risks that banks have to take into account, refer to the *Operational Risk Management* volume in this series.

Definition and Measures of Liquidity

The Basel Committee on Banking Supervision (BCBS) says liquidity is 'the ability of a bank to fund increases in assets and meet obligations as they come due, without incurring unacceptable losses'.[2] Banks make money by taking in short-term deposits by their clients and lending those funds out as longer-term loans. This discrepancy opens banks up to liquidity risk.

Regulators have not been blind to this risk for many decades; it was the bank runs of the Great Depression that exposed the dangers to the public of this discrepancy in the tenor of deposits and loans, not to mention other obligations and assets that may populate the balance sheets of banks and other authorised institutions (AIs). There is virtually no transaction or commitment that an AI might undertake that does not impact its liquidity position in some way. And, if the liquidity position of one bank or one institution is affected, so is the market as a whole. A shortfall of liquidity in one bank—imagine going to your bank and not having access to your money or a bank not having the cash to make interest payments—can have a massive impact on the financial system as a whole.

One lesson from the global financial crisis (GFC) is that banks and financial institutions may overlook the basic principles of liquidity risk management during good times, which leaves them exposed during times of crisis. Since 2008, regulators around the world have tightened up the frameworks under which they consider the adequacy of the liquidity position of individual institutions.

BCBS Principles for Managing Liquidity Risk

Much of the work of the BCBS, particularly in the aftermath of the GFC, has revolved around how financial institutions should manage their liquidity. Basel III, the latest series of agreements that guide most bank regulation around the world, includes a series of principles for the management and supervision of liquidity risk (Table 4.1). Basel III liquidity rules require banks to hold high quality liquid assets (HQLA) in their balance sheets.

The Basel III rules on capital management and liquidity management are being phased in over several years to 2019. While the aim of the rules is to make banks around the world stronger, at a very practical level abiding by the rules is a complex process.

---

[2] Basel Committee on Banking Supervision, 'Principles for Sound Liquidity Risk Management and Supervision', September 2008, p. 1.

TABLE 4.1 Basel Committee on Banking Supervision reforms - Basel III

Strengthens microprudential regulation and supervision, and adds a macroprudential overlay that includes capital buffers.

	Capital					Liquidity
	Pillar 1			Pillar 2	Pillar 3	Global liquidity standard and supervisory monitoring
	Capital	Risk coverage	Containing leverage	Risk management and supervision	Market discipline	

All Banks

Capital

Quality and level of capital
Greater focus on common equity. The minimum will be raised to 4.5% of risk-weighted assets, after deductions.

Capital loss absorption at the point of non-viability
Contractual terms of capital instruments will include a clause that allows – at the discretion of the relevant authority – write-off or conversion to common shares if the bank is judged to be non-viable. This principle increases the contribution of the private sector to resolving future banking crises and thereby reduces moral hazard.

Capital conservation buffer
Comprising common equity of 2.5% of risk-weighted assets, bringing the total common equity standard to 7%. Constraint on a bank's discretionary distributions will be imposed when banks fall into the buffer range.

Countercyclical buffer
Imposed within a range of 0–25% comprising common equity, when authorities judge credit growth is resulting in an unacceptable build up of systematic risk.

Risk coverage

Securitisations
Strengthens the capital treatment for certain complex securitisations. Requires banks to conduct more rigorous credit analyses of externally rated securitisation exposures.

Trading book
Significantly higher capital for trading and derivatives activities, as well as complex securitisations held in the trading book. Introduction of a stressed value-at-risk framework to help mitigate procyclicality. A capital charge for incremental risk that estimates the default and migration risks of unsecuritised credit products and takes liquidity into account.

Counterparty credit risk
Substantial strengthening of the counterparty credit risk framework. Includes: more stringent requirements for measuring exposure; capital incentives for banks to use central counterparties for derivatives; and higher capital for inter-financial sector exposures.

Bank exposures to central counterparties (CCPs)
The Committee has proposed that trade exposures to a qualifying CCP will receive a 2% risk weight and default fund exposures to a qualifying CCP will be capitalised according to a risk-based method that consistently and simply estimates risk arising from such default funds.

Containing leverage

Leverage ratio
A non-risk-based leverage ratio that includes off-balance sheet exposures will serve as a backstop to the risk-based capital requirement. Also helps contain system wide build up of leverage.

Risk management and supervision

Supplemental Pillar 2 requirements
Address firm-wide governance and risk management; capturing the risk of off-balance sheet exposures and securitisation activities; managing risk concentrations; providing incentives for banks to better manage risk and returns over the long term; sound compensation practices; valuation practices; stress testing; accounting standards for financial instruments; corporate governance; and supervisory colleges.

Market discipline

Revised Pillar 3 disclosures requirements
The requirements introduced relate to securitisation exposures and sponsorship of off-balance sheet vehicles. Enhanced disclosures on the detail of the components of regulatory capital and their reconciliation to the reported accounts will be required, including a comprehensive explanation of how a bank calculates its regulatory capital ratios.

Global liquidity standard and supervisory monitoring

Liquidity coverage ratio
The liquidity coverage ratio (LCR) will require banks to have sufficient high-quality liquid assets to withstand a 30-day stressed funding scenario that is specified by supervisors.

Net stable funding ratio
The net stable funding ratio (NSFR) is a longer-term structural ratio designed to address liquidity mismatches. It covers the entire balance sheet and provides incentives for banks to use stable sources of funding.

Principles for Sound Liquidity Risk Management and Supervision
The Committee's 2008 guidance *Principles for Sound Liquidity Risk Management and Supervision* takes account of lessons learned during the crisis and is based on a fundamental review of sound practices for managing liquidity risk in banking organisations.

Supervisory monitoring
The liquidity framework includes a common set of monitoring metrics to assist supervisors in identifying and analysing liquidity risk trends at both the bank and system-wide level.

SIFIs

In addition to meeting the Basel III requirements, global systemically important financial institutions (SIFIs) must have higher loss absorbency capacity to reflect the greater risks that they pose to the financial system. The Committee has developed a methodology that includes both quantitative indicators and qualitative elements to identify global systemically important banks (SIBs). The additional loss absorbency requirements are to be met with a progressive Common Equity Tier 1 (CET1) capital requirement ranging from 1% to 2.5%, depending on a bank's systemic importance. For banks facing the highest SIB surcharge, an additional loss absorbency of 1% could be applied as a disincentive to increase materially their global systemic importance in the future. A consultative document was developed in cooperation with the Financial Stability Board, which is coordinating the overall set of measures to reduce the moral hazard posed by global SIFIs.

Source: BCBS

The BCBS reforms include new rules for liquidity management. These rules are based on more stringent supervisory monitoring, the application of the 'Principles for Sound Liquidity Risk Management and Supervision' that the BCBS put forward in 2008 as well as greater monitoring of the liquidity coverage ratio (LCR) and the net stable funding ratio (NSFR).

The BCBS provides 15 principles for the management and supervision of liquidity risk.[3] The aim of these principles is to ensure that banks and other financial institutions always have enough liquidity at hand to cover their operating needs. The latest set of principles was put forward in September 2008, replacing the earlier 'Sound Practices for Managing Liquidity in Banking Organisations', that was put out in 2000.

The first and most fundamental of the BCBS principles on the management of liquidity risk makes it clear that banks are responsible for their liquidity and must manage any associated risks. This requires the creation of a strong internal management framework that takes into account possible losses as well as both secured and unsecured sources of funds. Regulators, for their part, are entrusted in ensuring that banks abide by the principles and maintain strong liquidity positions at all times.

Governance is a key consideration. Banks should be clear as to what their tolerance levels are and the liquidity needs of their particular business strategy. It is up to management to develop a strategy for liquidity management that matches the bank's strategy. What's more, both the tolerance levels and the management of liquidity should be constantly reviewed. Banks should also take into account the cost of liquidity when formulating a strategy—and remember that costs can change along with macro-economic environments.

Just as important is the development of a system to monitor and control risks associated with liquidity, or the lack of it. Cash flow projections are key, as are considerations of items such as forex values, changing interest rates and maturities or time horizons, all of which can have a sudden impact on liquidity. The general idea behind the BCBS principles is that there are no surprises and banks or other financial institutions always anticipate risk events—in other words, that they are ahead of, at least, the predictable developments in their operations.

This ability to predict, which is part of effective management of liquidity positions, should be visible in the short, medium and long terms. Banks should be just as prepared to manage intraday liquidity positions as they are to meet monthly or annual obligations, both under normal conditions and at times of stress. The BCBS principles underscore this requirement (Principle 8) as well as the requirement that collateral positions should be carefully managed and monitored, lest they become less valuable than the liability to which they are attached.

Three other considerations are also important. One is a requirement for banks and regulators to carry out regular stress tests, both at the institutional level and across the market. The need for bailouts in the United States during the GFC underscored the importance

---

[3] See Appendix A for the complete text of the BCBS's 'Principles for the management and supervision of liquidity risk'.

of such tests to avoid market meltdowns. A second is the need for banks and other AIs to have contingency funding plans that they can resort to in times of stress, particularly in modern times when regulators are less willing to step in to save institutions and the sums involved are increasingly large. A third is, ideally, to make the tests redundant and the need to implement contingency plans nothing more than a theoretical exercise—banks should have a cushion of 'unencumbered, high quality liquid assets to be held as insurance against a range of liquidity stress scenarios'.[4]

The BCBS principles deal with two other areas that are important for banks, financial institutions and the supervisory authorities that keep an eye on them. The first is regular public disclosures that allow for informed judgements about the soundness of a liquidity management approach of a particular institution. The second is the role of supervisors, who are expected to ensure sound management of liquidity across institutions through monitoring, testing, effective interventions before a risk event and, just as importantly, through regular communication with other regulators in different geographies.

Liquidity Coverage Ratio

The liquidity coverage ratio (LCR) measures the number of high quality liquid assets that banks have on hand to withstand a 30-day stressed funding scenario specified by supervisors. The BCBS revised the ratio in early 2013, issuing a new way to calculate it in January of that year. The LCR is a key component of the reforms ushered in with Basel III. In the period from 2015 to 2019, the minimum LCR requirement for banks should increase by 10% per year to 100%.[5]

The Hong Kong Monetary Authority (HKMA) started implementing the new LCR from 1 January 2015. The HKMA took a two-tiered approach to the LCR with Category 1 AIs, basically 12 large local licensed banks with liabilities above HK$250 billion, subject to the new ratio and 190 Category 2 AIs responsible to meet a pre-existing 25% liquidity ratio.

The aim of the LCR is to strengthen capital and liquidity regulations and shore up not only individual banks but also entire banking systems, the weaknesses of which have become clear in the years since 2008. The LCR was first published in 2010, along with a process to review the standard and a commitment to deal with unintended consequences quickly. The 2013 revision incorporated changes to the definition of high quality liquid assets (HQLA) and net cash outflows as well as a revised timetable for implementation.

The aim of the LCR is to make banks more resilient in the short term with access to enough liquidity—or assets that can be quickly converted into liquidity—to cover all its needs for 30 days.

---

[4] Basel Committee on Banking Supervision, 'Principles for Sound Liquidity Risk Management and Supervision', September 2008, p. 4.

[5] Basel Committee on Banking Supervision, 'Basel III: The Liquidity Coverage Ratio and liquidity risk monitoring tools', January 2013.

There are two parts to the LCR. The first is the value of the stock of a bank's HQLA and the other is the total net cash outflows. The LCR is expressed as:

$$\frac{Stock\ of\ HQLA}{Total\ net\ cash\ outflows\ over\ the\ next\ 30\ days} \geq 100\%$$

When it is fully implemented in 2019, banks and other financial institutions should have enough HQLA in hand to cover all their net cash outflows for 30 days. As of 2015, the LCR requirement under the BCBS standards was 60%, meaning that banks needed to have enough HQLA to cover 60% of their cash outflows for the period. The timetable from 2015 was as follows: in 2016, the ratio to rise to 70%, then 80% in 2017, 90% in 2018 and, finally, 100% in 2019.

There are two kinds of HQLA assets considered under the LCR.

Level 1 assets include cash, central bank reserves and some marketable securities backed by sovereigns and central banks. These assets are both high quality and very liquid and there is no limit on how many of these assets banks can hold to meet the requirements of the ratio.

Level 2 assets are of lower quality. They are further subdivided into Level 2A and Level 2B. Level 2A assets include some government securities, covered bonds and corporate securities. Level 2B assets include lower rated corporate bonds, residential mortgage backed securities and some equities that meet a few conditions. When counted in aggregate, Level 2 assets may not account for more than 40% of the HQLA that a bank counts towards the LCR. Level 2B assets may not account for more than 15% of the HQLA.

In turn, the total net outflows are defined as the total expected cash outflows minus the inflows under a specified stress scenario for 30 calendar days. The BCBS says the outflows should be calculated by multiplying the outstanding balances of various liabilities and off-balance-sheet commitments by the rates at which they are expected to be drawn down. Inflows are calculated by a similar but opposite process that counts inflows of cash and the rate at which they are expected. Cash inflows are subject to a cap of 75% of outflows, which ensures a minimum level of HQLA at all times.

Net Stable Funding Ratio

As part of its liquidity-focused reforms to develop a more resilient banking sector, the BCBS has also developed the Net Stable Funding Ratio (NSFR), which requires banks to 'maintain a stable funding profile in relation to the composition of their assets and off-balance-sheet activities'.[6] The NSFR is a longer-term structural ratio designed to address liquidity mismatches. It covers the entire balance sheet of a bank and provides incentives for banks to use stable sources of funding. The general idea is to limit risks

---

[6]Basel Committee on Banking Supervision, 'Basel III: The Net Stable Funding Ratio', January 2014.

associated with disruptions or changes to the regular sources of funding that a bank or other financial institution might have.

The mismatch that the BCBS sought to address with the NSFR is the lack of incentive for the private sector to limit too large a reliance on sources of funding that might be unstable, particularly during times of economic prosperity. Institutions that grow quickly during good times may not be prepared for the shocks of a sudden solvency crisis; and the interconnectedness of the financial system, and financial systems around the world, act as an amplifier to this risk. This was visible during 2007, when many banks easily met capital requirements in place at the time but were not able to properly manage their liquidity. Before the crisis, funding was both readily available and cheap but the conditions turned on a dime and the banking system was stressed beyond endurance. The result was institutional failures such as those of Bear Sterns or Lehman Brothers.

In looking for ways to avoid a repeat of those events, regulators started introducing the reforms proposed by the BCBS. These reforms centred around a set of standards to achieve two objectives. One, to ensure short-term resilience. That's where the LCR comes in. The second is to reduce funding risk over a longer time-frame by requiring banks to have enough stable sources of funding to mitigate risks, that gave way to the NSFR. The goal of the BCBS, and the regulators that support its reforms, is to ensure that the NSFR becomes a minimum standard by early 2018.

The NSFR is a measure of the amount of available 'stable' funding relative to the amount of required stable funding, and this ratio should be at least 100% on an on-going basis. The ratio is defined as:

$$\frac{Available\ amount\ of\ stable\ funding}{Required\ amount\ of\ stable\ funding} \geq 100\%$$

The difficulty in using this ratio, one that national regulators have to deal with, is determining what is a stable source of funding. This determination is made by considering source of funding through two parameters. The first is the 'funding tenor' and, for the purposes of the NSFR, the longer-term liabilities are generally considered more stable than short-term ones. The second is the 'funding type and counterparty' and operates under the assumption that deposits from retail customers and funding by small business customers are more stable than wholesale funding of the same maturity.

To determine how much stable funding banks require, the BCBS puts forward a number of criteria including stable funding for some proportion of lending to the real economy, the behaviour of banks and how they roll over maturing loans to preserve customers, the asset tenor that requires a smaller proportion of stable funding for short-dated assets, and the quality of assets and the value of liquidity with HQLA requiring less stable funding.

What is available stable funding (ASF)? The approach to determine what bank assets qualify as ASF is somewhat subjective and requires that banks assign a capital and liabilities to a particular category with a specific carrying value that is used to determine ASF. The amount assigned to each category is multiplied by an ASF factor and the total ASF is the sum of those amounts (see Table 4.2).

TABLE 4.2   Summary of Liability Categories and associated ASF Factors

ASF factor	Components of ASF category
100%	• Total regulatory capital • Other capital instruments and liabilities with effective residual maturity of one year or more
95%	• Stable non-maturity (demand) deposits and term deposits with residual maturity of less than one year provided by retail and SME customers
90%	• Less stable non-maturity deposits and term deposits with residual maturity of less than one year provided by retail and SME customers
50%	• Funding with residual maturity of less than one year provided by non-financial corporate customers • Operational deposits • Funding with residual maturity of less than one year from sovereigns, public sector entities (PSEs), and multilateral and national development banks • Other funding with residual maturity of not less than six months and less than one year not included in the above categories, including funding provided by central banks and financial institutions
0%	• All other liabilities and equity not included in above categories, including liabilities without a stated maturity • Derivatives payable net of derivatives receivable if payables are greater than receivables

In turn, the amount of required stable funding (RSF) is measured along similar lines but the considerations are slightly different. The aim of determining RSF is to arrive at a proximate figure of the amount of a particular asset that would have to be funded either because it is rolled over or because it could not be monetised. Encumbered assets, secured financing transaction and other assets are given different RSF factors (see Table 4.3).

A final consideration is off-balance-sheet exposure that requires little or no direct or immediate funding but can be a drain to long-term liquidity. The NSFR assigns an RSF factor to these activities that is either 5% or left up to national supervisors to determine.[7]

Determining Funding Needs

It is difficult to overestimate the importance of appropriately determining the funding needs that a bank or other financial institution might have. Banks are expected to be well funded, that is, to have enough funds at hand to cover their immediate liabilities. Every bank deposit is a liability as well as a trust. Clients trust that their money is where they put it and that they can access it at all times.

---

[7] For more details on how the various factors are calculated, see the BCBS discussion document 'Basel III: The Net Stable Funding Ratio' available at http://www.bis.org/publ/bcbs271.pdf.

TABLE 4.3   Summary of Asset Categories and Associated RSF Factors

RSF factor	Components of RSF category
0%	• Coins and banknotes • All central bank reserves • Unencumbered loans to banks subject to prudential supervision with residual maturities of less than six months
5%	• Unencumbered Level 1 assets, excluding coins, banknotes and central bank reserves
15%	• Unencumbered Level 2A assets
50%	• Unencumbered Level 2B assets • HQLA encumbered for a period of six months or more and less than one year • Loans to banks subject to prudential supervision with residual maturities six months or more and less than one year • Deposits held at other financial institutions for operational purposes • All other assets not included in the above categories with residual maturity of less than one year, including loans to non-bank financial institutions, loans to non-financial corporate clients, loans to retail and small business customers, and loans to sovereigns, central banks and PSEs
65%	• Unencumbered residential mortgages with a residual maturity of one year or more and with a risk weight of less than or equal to 35% • Other unencumbered loans not included in the above categories, excluding loans to financial institutions, with a residual maturity of one year or more and with a risk weight of less than or equal to 35% under the Standardised Approach
85%	• Other unencumbered performing loans with risk weights greater than 35% under the Standardised Approach and residual maturities of one year or more, excluding loans to financial institutions • Unencumbered securities that are not in default and do not qualify as HQLA including exchange-traded equities • Physical traded commodities, including gold
100%	• All assets that are encumbered for a period of one year or more • Derivatives receivable net of derivatives payable if receivables are greater than payables • All other assets not included in the above categories, including non-performing loans, loans to financial institutions with a residual maturity of one year or more, non-exchange-traded equities, fixed assets, pension assets, intangibles, deferred tax assets, retained interest, insurance assets, subsidiary interests, and defaulted securities

Source: BCBS

The Asset and Liability Management Committee (ALCO) is a risk management committee made up of senior management executives. Its primary goal is to evaluate, monitor and approve the various practices of the bank with a view to the risk they pose of creating imbalances in the bank's capital structure. In other words, the ALCO is key to ensuring that banks and other AIs are well funded. They do this by setting limits on arbitrage borrowing in short-term markets and ensuring an appropriate level of long-term instruments. They look at liquidity risk, interest rate risk, operational risk and the possibility of external events that could affect future funding needs and the strategic allocations in the bank's balance sheet.

The ALCO is an important piece of the machine that banks use to determine funding needs, but it is not the only one. Financial institutions also rely on a series of other tools, some of which are handed to them by regulators and others by common sense, established practice or the standards set by the BCBS. Among these tools that help ensure banks better determine their funding needs are reserve requirement ratios, analysis of loan and deposit trends, careful consideration of the liquidity gap and liquidity planning.

Reserve Requirement Ratios

In late August 2015, the People's Bank of China (PBOC) reduced the reserve requirement ratio (RRR) for Mainland China's banks by 50 basis points to 18%. It was the third time the PBOC cut the RRR in the year. Mainland China's central bank has long used the RRR as a tool to manage the amount of liquidity in the financial system. By lowering the RRR, it allows banks to lend out more of their capital, thus increasing the amount of cash in the economy and, hopefully, economic growth.

Other regulators also rely on the RRR to influence interest rates. In the US, for example, reserve requirements are one of several tools that include open market operations (basically buying or selling treasury bonds), the discount rate at which the US Federal Reserve lends money to banks and the more nuanced tool of verbal persuasion.

The RRR is the portion of depositors' balances that banks have to keep on hand as cash or cash equivalents, basically capital in reserve. Banks may hold excess reserves but the RRR determines the minimum amount that they should hold. These reserves are included in a bank's balance sheet but they are not used to fund loans. A very simple equation to describe how the ratio impacts a bank's balance sheet is:

$$Total\ Deposits = \frac{Reserves * 1}{(R + E)}$$

In this case, the 'R' refers to the RRR and the 'E' to the excess reserve ratio of the bank in question. This formula is useful in determining the total deposits that a bank has and can also be used to determine the portion of those deposits that it can realistically lend out.

National regulators set the ratio to both ensure the strength of banks and to meet national monetary goals. As we discussed above, the RRR is a useful and relatively effective tool to add or take away liquidity from the market. Mainland China's move in August 2015 to cut the RRR by 0.5% added as much as RMB1.2 trillion in liquidity to the economy, for example.

Not all countries use RRR. Hong Kong, for example, follows the BCBS principles and relies instead on the capital and liquidity adequacy principles based on the LCR and the NSFR, among others. Other countries like Canada, Sweden, Australia and New Zealand have also abolished the traditional RRR. Rather, banks are increasingly relying on the risk-based capital requirements that the BCBS puts forward. The LCR is not unlike the traditional RRR, although it takes into consideration the quality of assets that banks hold.

In 2014, the HKMA encouraged banks in Hong Kong to keep higher levels of reserves than those required by the BCBS standards, even though most banks in the Special Administrative Region typically maintain capital adequacy ratios already well above those required by the Basel committee.

Loan and Deposit Trends

But how do banks determine their funding needs on an ongoing basis? Modern financial institutions are complex conglomerates with dozens of business lines, hundreds or thousands of branches, multiple subsidiaries and enough operational departments to make any observer dizzy. Managing this complexity can be a Herculean task. A key function is to analyse loan and deposit trends and use this analysis as part of a liquidity management strategy that shifts along with market conditions.

Banks and banking executives, economists, analysts and regulators pay close attention to loan and deposit trends and the loan to deposit ratio both in individual institutions and the financial system as a whole.

Take, for example, the month of June 2014 in Hong Kong (not for any particular reason). That month, according to the HKMA's monetary statistics, loans grew 1.6% month-on-month while deposits grew just 0.9% month-on-month. The impact of this is counterintuitive. In effect, the assets of the banks and financial institutions in the system (the loans) rose by almost twice as much as the liabilities (the deposits). That month, the loan to deposit ratio across the whole system rose to 73.6%, up from 73.1% a month earlier.

This change was happening just as regulators put more emphasis on banks having enough sources of stable funding to support both their growth and the amount of liquidity. The upshot was the likelihood of higher funding costs for banks.

The HKMA keeps careful tabs on these trends and adjusts the allowable loan to deposit ratio accordingly. Since 2013, the HKMA expects authorised institutions to have enough stable sources of funding to match the maturity of both loans and deposits. The move followed a spike in loans issued across Hong Kong and the possibility of banks stretching themselves too thin. The fear was the banks were supporting their lending activities through short-term funding and were not fully prepared for a squeeze in the event of a bank run.

The lesson for banks is relatively simple, but not always easy to manage: they should ensure enough funding is in place to sustain growth. A traditionally conservative regulator, the HKMA was working to ensure banks in Hong Kong did not end up with a negative liquidity gap that could pose a risk to their operations, threaten client funds or jeopardise the system as a whole.

Liquidity Gap

A liquidity gap is the difference between the assets and liabilities that a bank—or any firm, really—has. This gap is caused by the different properties that assets and liabilities might have. It can be positive or negative, depending on the balance sheet of a particular institution. The aim of effective liquidity planning is to ensure a positive gap at all times. The liquidity gap is, by its very nature, very volatile. It changes throughout every operating day as deposits and withdrawals are made or obligations met. The liquidity gap offers a quick look at the risk profile of a bank.

Despite its nature as a relatively short-term instrument, liquidity gap analysis is commonly used as the basis for scenario analysis and stress tests. ALM teams can, for example, track gap risk exposure by using maturity and cash-flow mismatches, taking into account not only the maturity dates of assets and liabilities but, just as importantly, intermediate cash flow position by testing for loan prepayments, for example, or the unforeseen use of lines of credit.

How do banks do this? The first step is to determine the length and number of each time interval to be used. The next is to define the maturities of both assets and liabilities, ideally by taking into account both normal and stress conditions. For assets that don't mature such as credit card balances, for example, teams make some assumptions based on historical trends. The next step is to put every asset and every liability into an appropriate time slot. The aim of this analysis is to avoid any imbalances by adapting the bank's future strategy to the actual and predicted conditions and the size and nature of the liquidity gap.

Liquidity Planning

Effective liquidity planning is a recurrent theme for the BCBS, and regulators who follow the Basel Committee's standards. Banks should have carefully crafted liquidity plans in place. It is up to regulators to evaluate the liquidity plans of individual institutions and to intervene quickly to deal with any deficiencies that could jeopardise the institutions themselves, and the financial system as a whole. This intervention could take many forms, from requiring that institutions strengthen their liquidity management practices—such as their internal policies, controls and reporting—to requiring that banks improve their contingency planning or lower their liquidity risk by keeping greater reserves. At other times, the regulator can block institutions from making acquisitions that could risk the systemic access to liquidity.

At its very core, the aim of liquidity planning is to put in place a strong liquidity framework that can withstand risk events. Both the board of directors and senior management should understand the risks that the institution faces and the strategies in place to deal with risk and the eventual risk event. Stress testing plays a key role in setting up these plans.

Another important component of an effective liquidity plan is to be ready for contingencies. Common sense dictates that any liquidity contingency plan goes hand in hand with plans to ensure adequate access to capital. Contingency planning should take into account changing conditions, including higher costs of liquidity or difficulties in accessing it in the event of changing conditions.

A third factor to consider is the relationship and interplay between assets, liabilities, liquidity and capital. Since the GFC, more banks have committees to manage their balance sheets, with senior executives at the helm. The ALCO may report to this higher level committee. Its goal is to effectively manage this interplay and to bring all data together for analysis under one umbrella, so to speak.

New data management tools makes this process somewhat easier, or at least faster. Banks and other financial institutions are more complex than ever before but the tools exist to manage this complexity more efficiently.

Funds Transfer Pricing

Funds transfer pricing (FTP) is one approach that banks can use to measure how each individual source of funds contributes to overall profitability. Banks often use FTP to identify strengths and weaknesses in terms of funding in their organisation. To be effective and balanced, an ALM strategy has to rely on a diversified funding base, and this means that FTP is necessary, particularly when a company has multiple divisions, or hundreds in the case of a large bank. FTP is a key tool to manage liquidity risk within a bank's balance sheet.

It is very difficult, in practical terms, to completely neutralise risk exposures. The constant cycle of crises would seem to amply make this point. One thing banks, or the various businesses within them, can do is ensure they obtain funds at a rate that matches their ALM needs. This internal funding rate can then be described as 'the rate at which a business line obtains its funds'.[8]

There are two main reasons why a carefully crafted FTP strategy is important. One is that it enforces a certain discipline and risk control within a business. The second is that it has a direct impact on the returns that a particular line of business can generate.

The FTP mechanism operates as part of a larger risk management structure that considers both assets and liabilities and is, generally, centralised within Treasury operations. Given the complicated balance sheets of most banks, a number of risks are immediately visible. A couple of such risks can be partially addressed through an effective FTP mechanism. The first is interest rate risk. Interest rates fluctuate daily, which means that the daily liabilities of particular units could also fluctuate daily, each of these units requires an internal source of funds that is responsive enough to deal with these daily fluctuations.

---

[8]Dalessandro, A. (2013) *Effective Strategies for Assets and Liabilities Management.*

A second type of risk is liquidity risk. Most bank units require that their assets be constantly funded and that the funding be continuous and rolling; again, this requires an effective FTP mechanism.

An effective FTP mechanism should also take into account capital reserve requirements, not necessarily just meeting the daily needs of units but ensuring their proper capitalisation. But implementing an FTP strategy can be challenging due to both regulatory constraints and internal controls at banks. At the heart of an effective FTP strategy is the idea that the costs of risk that appear in ALM are charged explicitly to businesses, products or customers, and tracked by the Treasury.

This internal funding structure helps better manage liquidity and liquidity risk for each business line, all the while minimising risk exposures. In short, as Anthony Dalessandro explains, FTP helps banks centralise both the measurement and management of interest rate risk, ensure consistent product pricing guidelines for business lines, set profitability targets and measure the profitability of business units independently of interest rate risk.

But to do all this, FTP has to be implemented in a curve that moves along with changes in interest rates and the needs of individual business units. It has to take into account liquidity mismatches, the potential cost of liquidity risk and such diverse items as forex risks or capital controls.

Stress Tests

Stress tests are key ways for regulators to ensure the strength of their banking sectors. They can help determine whether banks are strong enough to make it through financial and economic crisis without bending or breaking. In carrying out stress tests, regulators identify risk factors and possible events that can affect the credit worthiness of banks and other institutions.

The US Federal Reserve, for example, instituted a Comprehensive Liquidity Analysis and Review mechanism in 2012 for the largest banks. The mechanism is, basically, a series of stress tests.

It is important not just to carry out the stress tests but for both banks and regulators to use the results to strengthen liquidity plans and the banking system as a whole. Institutions should use the tests to determine their strategy and tactics to shore up their liquidity risk planning and be in a better position to deal with events of liquidity stress. Tests should take into account not only multiple scenarios but also different time horizons and changes in the economic and systemic context.

The aim of stress tests is for banks to analyse how their operations and plans would hold up under different scenarios and how different events would impact each unit and the institutional group, particularly given that business lines are often intertwined. By carrying out stress tests banks may better understand where the risks are and how risk events could affect them. The results of a particular test could help both the bank and the regulatory authority to determine if more tests are needed or whether tests on individual business lines, branches or subsidiaries are warranted.

The extent and frequency of the stress tests should vary depending on the size of a bank and its liquidity exposure as well as changing conditions. Since the introduction of Basel III, banks have been encouraged to build into their systems the ability to carry out more frequent tests, particularly when circumstances change, market conditions become more volatile or when regulators request them.

Banks should also consider that their operations are never in a bubble. Counter-parties, both competing institutions and clients, typically respond to risk events and these responses should be considered.

Under normal circumstances stress tests should consider events that are relatively common in markets, such as a drying up of liquidity, constrained accessing of secured and unsecured funding, existing restriction on currency convertibility and disruptions to the operations of payment or settlement systems that could be caused by a wide variety of incidents from changes to regulations to market sentiment or even natural disasters. Some events may not only limit access to liquidity but could also lead to a surge in the amount of liquidity that is required over a short period of time. A particularly important consideration is the link between market liquidity and any constraints on funding liquidity, particularly for banks that rely on a specific funding market.

The BCBS outlines a number of assumptions that banks should use in stress tests, including:[9]

- asset liquidity and an erosion in the value of liquid assets;
- run-off of retail funding;
- availability of funding sources, both secured and unsecured;
- the correlation between funding markets and diversification of funding sources;
- margin calls and collateral requirements;
- funding tenors;
- potential draws on committed lines of credit;
- liquidity taken up by off-balance-sheet activities;
- availability of lines extended to the bank;
- credit rating triggers;
- FX convertibility and access to markets;
- the ability to transfer liquidity across entities, sectors and borders;
- access to central bank facilities;
- the bank's operational ability to monetise assets;
- remedial actions in place and the ability of the bank to execute them; and
- estimates of future balance sheet growth.

---

[9] Basel Committee on Banking Supervision, 'Principles for Sound Liquidity Risk Management and Supervision', September 2008, p. 26.

Stress tests based on the normal course of business are important, but rarely do institutions fail under such conditions. It is when conditions change that liquidity plans are tried. When designing stress tests, banks should consider abnormal circumstances, using historical context and stretching that out. The liquidity position of a bank or other financial institution can be rapidly affected during a crisis and, to be effective, stress testing should take crisis scenarios under consideration as well.

Summary

- Liquidity is key to the operations of banks and other financial institutions. The need for liquidity may, at times, override profitability when it comes to planning the future of a bank.
- Effective liquidity controls are a key component of effective asset and liability management (BALM).
- Liquidity risk is the risk that a bank or other authorised institution (AI) may be unable to meet its obligations as they fall due.
- There is virtually no transaction or commitment that an AI might undertake that does not impact its liquidity position in some way. And, if the liquidity position of one bank or one institution is affected, so is the market as a whole.
- Basel III, the latest series of agreements that guide most bank regulation around the world, includes a set of principles for the management and supervision of liquidity risk. Basel III liquidity rules require banks to hold high quality liquid assets (HQLA) in their balance sheets. These assets are usually linked to fixed income, currency and commodity (FICC) products that may be less profitable than riskier over the counter (OTC) products or derivatives.
- The Basel III rules on capital management and liquidity management are being phased in over several years to 2017. The BCBS provides 15 principles for the management and supervision of liquidity risk.
- The liquidity coverage ratio (LCR) measures the amount of high quality liquid assets that banks have on hand to withstand a 30-day stressed funding scenario specified by supervisors. The Hong Kong Monetary Authority (HKMA) started implementing the new LCR from 1 January 2015.
- The aim of the LCR is to strengthen capital and liquidity regulations and shore up not only individual banks but also entire banking systems, the weaknesses of which have become clear since 2008.
- There are two kinds of HQLA assets considered under the LCR. Level 1 assets include cash, central bank reserves and some marketable securities backed by sovereigns and central banks. Level 2 assets are of lower quality. They are further subdivided into Level 2A and Level 2B. Level 2A assets include some government securities, covered bonds and corporate securities.

- The Net Stable Funding Ratio (NSFR) requires banks to 'maintain a stable funding profile in relation to the composition of their assets and off-balance-sheet activities'.
- The Asset-Liability Committee (ALCO) is a risk management committee made up of senior management executives. Its primary goal is to evaluate, monitor and approve the various practices of the bank with a view to the risk they pose of creating imbalances in the bank's capital structure. In other words, the ALCO is key to ensuring that banks and other AIs are well funded.
- The reserve requirement ratio (RRR) is the portion of depositors' balances that banks have to keep on hand as cash or cash equivalents, basically capital in reserve. Banks may hold excess reserves but the RRR determines the minimum amount that they should hold. Not many regulators still use the RRR, having switched to the LCR and the NSFR, instead.
- A liquidity gap is the difference between the assets and liabilities that a bank—or any firm, really—has. This gap is caused by the different properties that assets and liabilities might have. It can be positive or negative, depending on the balance sheet of a particular institution. The aim of effective liquidity planning is to ensure a positive gap at all times.
- Funds transfer pricing (FTP) is used to measure how every individual source of funds contributes to overall profitability. Banks often use FTP to identify strengths and weaknesses in terms of funding in their organisation. FTP is a key tool to manage liquidity risk within a bank's balance sheet.
- Stress tests are key ways for regulators to ensure the strength of their banking sectors. They can help determine whether banks are strong enough to make it through financial and economic crisis without bending or breaking. In carrying out stress tests, regulators identify risk factors and possible events that can affect the credit worthiness of banks and other institutions.

Key Terms

Asset and Liability Management
   Committee (ALCO)
Asset and liability management (ALM)
Available stable funding (ASF)
Basel III
Basel Committee on Banking Supervision
   (BCBS)
Deposits
Fixed income, currency and commodity
   (FICC)
Funding
Funds transfer pricing (FTP)
Global financial crisis

High Quality Liquid Assets (HQLA)
Hong Kong Monetary Authority (HKMA)
Liquidity
Liquidity Coverage Ratio (LCR)
Liquidity gap
Liquidity planning
Liquidity risk
Loans
Net Stable Funding Ratio (NSFR)
Over the counter (OTC)
Reserve requirement ratios (RRR)
Stress tests
US Federal Reserve

Review Questions

1. Define and explain the two key ratios that the Basel Committee on Banking Supervision (BCBS) uses to help banks and regulators ensure adequate levels of liquidity.
2. What is a liquidity gap? How does it affect liquidity planning?
3. What is the reserve requirement ratio (RRR) and what purpose does it serve?
4. How do stress tests help shore up the banking system?

Further Reading

Basel Committee on Banking Supervision, 'Principles for Sound Liquidity Risk Management and Supervision', September 2008.

Basel Committee on Banking Supervision, 'Basel III: The Liquidity Coverage Ratio and liquidity risk monitoring tools'. April 2013. http://www.bis.org/publ/bcbs238.pdf.

Basel Committee on Banking Supervision, 'Basel III: The Net Stable Funding Ratio'. January 2014. http://www.bis.org/publ/bcbs271.pdf.

Basel Committee on Banking Supervision, 'Assessment of Basel III LCR regulations: Hong Kong SAR'. March 2015. http://www.bis.org/bcbs/publ/d314.pdf.

Hong Kong Institute of Bankers (2013) *Operational Risk Management*, Singapore: John Wiley & Sons.

Hong Kong Monetary Authority, 'Supervisory Policy Manual: LM1 – Regulatory Framework for Supervision of Liquidity Risk', July 2016.

Managing Interest Rate Risk

After studying this chapter, you should be able to:

1 Explain the different types of interest rate risk.

2 Explain the various tools that banks use to analyse and mitigate interest rate risk such as interest rate gap analysis, duration analysis and net interest income sensitivity analysis.

3 Describe some of the approaches that banks can use to minimise interest rate risk such as immunisation, hedging and securitisation.

Introduction

The level, changes and forecast of changes in interest rates are important considerations for the effective management of bank assets and liabilities. The Basel Committee on Banking Supervision (BCBS) regularly highlights their importance through documents and consultations and includes interest rate risk as a key part of the Pillar 2 framework of its banking standards.[1] As of 2015, the BCBS suggested that a stronger framework for the management of interest rate risk may be necessary for banks around the world.

Interest income represents a huge portion of the total income of most banks in Hong Kong and other developed markets, often more than half. As a result, understanding and managing the risks associated with changes in interest rates is a particularly important function to ensure the stability and strength of the banks that make up the financial system.

This chapter discusses interest rate risk and the tools that banks have at their disposal to manage such risk. The discussion starts with a look at the various categories of interest rate risk and how they affect asset and liability management operations at banks. The discussion then moves on to interest rate gap analysis and its importance in the management of bank assets and liabilities as well as a brief discussion of the limitations of gap analysis. The next section provides a primer for duration analysis and how it is used to quantify risk associated with interest rates as well as the practical applications of the duration gap. We pause for a very brief look at basis point value before moving on to the more weighty topic of immunisation and hedging of interest rate risk. The last two sections offer a big picture look at net interest income sensitivity analysis and the use of securitisation in managing interest rate risk.

Types of Interest Rate Risk

Banks and other financial institutions are exposed to interest rate risk through several of their business activities, including lending and taking deposits, as well as foreign exchange transactions. Most banks accept some kind of interest rate risk but are aware that this type of risk poses a danger to both earnings and capital adequacy. The HKMA suggests institutions have processes in place to identify, measure, monitor and manage interest rate risk.[2]

Interest rate risk in the banking book (IRRBB) is a key component of the Basel capital framework. IRRBB 'refers to the current or prospective risk to the bank's capital and earnings arising from adverse movements in interest rates that affect the bank's banking

---

[1] The BCBS issued a consultative document on 'Interest rate risk in the banking book' as part of efforts to strengthen supervision of how banks manage such risks.

[2] Hong Kong Monetary Authority. 'Supervisory Policy Manual: Interest Rate Risk Management.' 13 December 2002.

book positions,' notes the BCBS in a 2016 paper.[3] Changes in interest rates can lead to changes in the present value and the timing for cash flows which, in turn, change the value of the assets, liabilities and off-balance-sheet items of a bank and its economic value. Changes in interest rates affect the earnings of a bank by causing changes in income and expense and directly impacting net interest income (NII). Ultimately, too much IRRBB can threaten the capital base or the earnings of a bank, or both.

There are three main sub-types of IRRBB that BCBS identifies. The first is gap risk, which 'arises from the term structure of banking book instruments' and refers to the risk associated with the timing in the change of rates of various instruments. The second is basis risk or 'the impact of relative changes in interest rates for financial instruments that have similar tenors but are priced using different interest rate indices'. The third is option risk, which stems from 'option derivative position or from optional elements in a bank's assets, liabilities and/or off-balance-sheet items, where the bank or its customer can alter the level and timing of their cash flows.'

Taking these types of risk into account and preparing for them, both in terms of the long-term profitability of the bank as well as its short-term liquidity position, are important considerations for effective ALM.

There are different ways to manage interest rate risk; the HKMA says that 'policies, procedures and limits … should be properly documented, drawn up after careful consideration of interest rate risk associated with different types of lending, and reviewed and approved by management at the appropriate level.'[4] An information system that is accurate and timely is key to managing this type of risk and the policies should be included in the internal risk control manual.[5]

Interest Rate Gap Analysis

Gap analysis is a statistical measure of the risk that is commonly associated with targets for net interest income (or margins). It is commonly used to assess both interest rate risk and liquidity risk. Banks started using gap analysis widely in the 1980s to manage interest risk and as a complement to duration analysis. Analysing the interest rate gap is not unlike analysing the liquidity gap, the aim is to avoid a negative gap.

As with most tools, the underlying idea is not complicated. Gap analysis considers simple maturity and repricing scheduled to generate indicators of the sensitivity to changing interest rates of an institution's interest rate risk position and its value. A typical

---

[3] Basel Committee on Banking Supervision. 'Standards: Interest rate risk in the banking book'. Bank for International Settlements. April 2016.

[4] Hong Kong Monetary Authority. 'Supervisory Policy Manual: Interest Rate Risk Management.' 13 December 2012. p. 15.

[5] For a more in-depth discussion of interest rate risk, refer to the *Treasury Management Operations* book in this series.

gap analysis evaluates the exposure of earnings to interest rate or liquidity risk by deducting interest-rate-sensitive liabilities over several time intervals from the corresponding interest-rate-sensitive assets to arrive at a repricing gap for each time period. The gap is then multiplied by an expected change in interest rates to determine an approximation of the change in net interest income caused by the expected change in rates.

The analysis includes an assumption of the change in interest rates. This assumption is typically based on various factors including historical experience, simulations of potential interest rate movements by regulators and the judgement of bank management.

An extension of traditional gap analysis is earnings sensitivity analysis, which focuses on changes to the earnings of a bank due to changes in interest rates and the composition of its balance sheet.

A first step in carrying out a traditional static gap analysis is to develop a forecast for the movement of interest rates. The next step is to select a series of 'time buckets' or intervals to determine when assets and liabilities will be repriced, and group the various assets and liabilities in the bank's balance sheet into these buckets. The next step is to calculate the interest rate gap for each bucket and, finally, forecast the next interest income given the assumed changes to interest rates (See Table 5.1).

Let's look at a simplified example of how banks may use gap analysis to measure their interest rate risk. Imagine that a banks extends a $100,000 four-year car loan to one of its customers at a fixed rate of 8.5%. The bank gets the funds for the loan through a one-year $100,000 note for which it pays 4.5%. This means that the bank's initial spread is 4% (8.5% – 4.5%). Gap analysis does not look at the spread but at the bank's risk. Going forward, the bank's income is capped at 8.5% but its liabilities (the amount it pays on the original note) could change. Imagine an increase of 50 basis points on the cost of the original note, which could translate into the bank paying 5% for the funds and narrower spread of just 3.5%. While this may not look like much, consider that it is 12.5% less. The risk to the bank's balance sheet of such a small change in interest rates is significant.

TABLE 5.1   Summary of gap and the change in the NII

	Gap Summary				
Gap	Change in Interest Income	Change in Interest Income		Change in Interest Expense	Change in Net Interest Income
Positive	Increase	Increase	>	Increase	Increase
Positive	Decrease	Decrease	>	Decrease	Decrease
Negative	Increase	Increase	<	Increase	Decrease
Negative	Decrease	Decrease	<	Decrease	Increase
Zero	Increase	Increase	=	Increase	None
Zero	Decrease	Decrease	=	Decrease	None

Limitations of Traditional Gap Analysis

Gap analysis, in short, measures the volume of rate-sensitive assets minus the volume of rate-sensitive liabilities. The traditional and static gap analysis contrasts the sensitivity to changes in interest rates of both assets and liabilities with an eye to managing net interest income. This is both necessary and useful information but it makes for an approach that is far from foolproof. There are a number of limitations to this traditional gap analysis.

At the top of the list is the fact that gap analysis relies on a series of assumptions about upcoming changes to interest rate. These assumptions are, of course, based on the best possible information available as well as constant contact with regulators. Nevertheless, it can be of limited use in the event of rapid changes to macroeconomic conditions that lead to unexpected fluctuations in rates. Hong Kong, in particular, is a very open economy that is dependent on both China for much of its growth and the United States, because the Hong Kong dollar (HKD) is pegged to the USD. Rapid changes in one or the other, as was the case in the beginning of 2016 when markets crashed in Mainland China, can lead to unexpected movements in Hong Kong rates.

A second limitation is that the assumptions used in gap analysis are also based on the estimations of bank management. Making these assumptions is a risky proposition in itself, because it assumes that the bank can predict movement in rates better than the market. Gap analysis considers a single moment in time. Interbank rates, for example, can change by the minute and certainly on a daily basis, so the analysis can be obsolete by the time it is complete. There is really no set timeframe for changes in rates, some years they change weekly and other years they don't change at all. This opens the door for a series of errors that emerge after the fact.

A third limitation is caused by the link between rates and the value of foreign exchange. A comprehensive analysis of interest rate risk should certainly take the value of the various currencies used to denominate the many different instruments and currencies that a bank may hold. Nevertheless, the relative returns or liabilities associated with foreign currency instruments are definitely impacted by changes in the value of those currencies. Currency values can not only change very fast, they can also change independently of the level of interest rates set by regulators or the market. Gap analysis does not consider the cumulative impact of changes in interest rates on the risk position of a bank.

A fourth problem is that gap analysis offers a glimpse of the interest rate risk exposure of a bank but there are multiple factors that affect the net interest income, such as the level of interest rates, changes in the mix of assets and liabilities that the bank holds and the volume of assets and liabilities outstanding, changes in the relationship between yields from assets and rates that banks pay on their liabilities. Not all these factors can be controlled.

A fifth concern is that gap analysis basically ignores the time value of money. The maturity buckets upon which the analysis is based do not really differentiate between cash that flows in at the beginning of the time period versus the cash that flows in at the end. This is not accurate.

Another issue is that gap analysis often overlooks liabilities that do not pay any interest, which some banks allocate as non-rate-sensitive. Gap analysis, for example, does not consider rate risk associated with demand deposit flows, even though deposits may drop when interest rates rise because the opportunity cost of demand deposits rises for customers. A way to compensate is to allocate demand deposits that are rate sensitive to the appropriate time bucket.

A seventh and final concern is that gap analysis does not take into account the risk linked to options that are included in loans, securities or deposits, such as prepayment options in mortgages that borrowers might take up in the event of a drop in interest rates. These options all have different values and represent different levels of risk. When customers exercise these options, they are altering the effective value of gap.[6]

Duration Analysis

An important factor in determining interest rate risk is the amount of time that capital is committed to a particular investment product. The tool that banks and other financial institutions use to quantify this risk is duration analysis, with the duration being the average time period of a capital commitment. The duration is also called the Macaulay duration.

The duration is a measure that considers the maturity of a particular security of investment vehicle using a weighted average of the present values of cash flows.

It can be used to measure elasticity based on the maturity date—the time that passes until the final payment. Duration does incorporate the timing and size of cash flows but is more interesting to measure how sensitive a particular security is to changes in interest rates. In effect, duration is an approximate measure of the price elasticity of demand. This elasticity can be determined using the following formula:

$$Price\ Elasticity\ of\ Demand = -\frac{\%\ Change\ in\ Quantity\ Demanded}{\%\ Change\ in\ Price}$$

There is a correlation between the duration of a security and the impact of a change in interest rates. The longer the duration, the larger the change in price for a given change in interest rates. Once again, some math is required to measure this impact:

$$Duration \cong -\frac{\frac{\Delta P}{P}}{\frac{\Delta i}{(1+i)}}$$

---

[6]Timothy W. Koch and S. Scott MacDonald: 'Bank Management'. South-Western, Cengage Learning. Ohio, United States. 2010. 262–267.

In effect, duration is a weighted average of the time until the expected cash flows from a security will be received relative to the price of the security. It is useful to determine the risk of a particular security actually being turned into a losing proposition in the (generally likely) event of changes in interest rates. At times of rising interest rates, this calculation is particularly important. One variant of this duration calculation is the modified duration which is useful to arrive at an estimate of price volatility.

Another important variant of this duration calculation is the effective duration, which is calculated as:

$$Effective\ Duration = \frac{P_{i-} - P_{i+}}{P_0(i^+ - i^-)}$$

To summarise, duration analysis looks at the average life of a financial instrument. A duration analysis is started by comparing the individual duration of each asset and each liability of a financial institution and is constructed in a way that allows a financial institution to measure the interest rate sensitivity of each asset and liability or of whole portfolios. The ultimate aim of duration analysis is to immunise portfolios and better manage risk.

Practical Applications of Duration Gap

Measuring the duration of various instruments or of the assets and liabilities of a bank can be used to determine the duration gap, which indicates the impact of changes in interest rates on the net worth of a financial institutions.

Measuring the duration gap in a particular security or a portfolio of securities is necessary to prevent significant impact from interest rate risk events, such as rapid changes in the interest rate environment caused by changes in macroeconomic conditions or the amount of liquidity in the market.

There are a number of steps necessary to analyse the duration gap. The first is to forecast interest rates. The second is to estimate the market value of bank assets, liabilities and the equity that stockholders have. The next step is to estimate the weighted average duration of assets and liabilities, incorporating the effects of both on and off-balance-sheet items. Finally, forecast changes in the market value of stockholders' equity in different interest rate environments.

A positive duration gap suggest that assets are, on average, more price sensitive than liabilities so when interest rates rise, the value of assets falls proportionally more in value than liabilities and EVE falls accordingly, and vice versa. A negative duration gap suggests the opposite, that liabilities are more price sensitive than weighted assets so when interest rates fall, assets fall less than liabilities and EVE rises (see Table 5.2).

There are a number of practical applications for duration analysis and the duration gap but the most obvious one is to determine when a particular security, such as a bond, will become profitable. One way to look at this is to consider the duration of a zero coupon bond. By definition, the duration of such a bond is equal to its maturity.

TABLE 5.2   DGAP Summary

		DGAP Summary					
DGAP	**Change in Interest Rates**	**Assets**		**Liabilities**		**Equity**	
Positive	Increase	Decrease	>	Decrease	→	Decrease	
Positive	Decrease	Increase	>	Increase	→	Increase	
Negative	Increase	Decrease	<	Decrease	→	Increase	
Negative	Decrease	Increase	<	Increase	→	Decrease	
Zero	Increase	Decrease	=	Decrease	→	None	
Zero	Decrease	Increase	=	Increase	→	None	

The effective duration of a security is used to, for example, estimate the price sensitivity of a security when it contains embedded options. Another use is to compare the estimated price of a security in a falling interest rate environment against its price in a rising environment.

There are some practical implications to this.

Duration analysis can be used to consider the duration gap, which focuses on managing the market value of, for example, stockholders' equity. The duration gap compares the duration of a bank's assets with the duration of the bank's liabilities and examines the impact of changes in interest rate to the value of the equity that shareholders have. A bank can use the duration gap to protect either the market value of its equity or its net interest income but not both. The duration gap analysis focuses on the impact on equity of changes in interest rates.

Changes in interest rates typically require banks to react by reinvesting cash flows from assets or refinance rolled-over liabilities at different interest rates. An increase in rates may boost the return on the assets that a bank holds but also increases the bank's costs by making funds more expensive.

There are a few other risks that can be analysed using the duration gap. One is reinvestment rate risk. If interest rates rise, the yield from any reinvestment of cash flows rises along with the rates and the holding period return (HPR) increases with it. The opposite is also true. If interest rates fall, the yield from a security also falls and the HPR decreases. Another risk that can be analysed is price risk. Once again, if interest rates rise prices also rise, which means that selling a security prior to maturity translates into a rise in HPR. Again, the opposite is also true. Ultimately, increases in interest rates will boost the HPR from a higher reinvestment rate but reduce it from capital losses if a security is sold before maturity. Conversely, if interest rates decrease, so will the HPR from a lower reinvestment rate but increase it from capital gains in the event that the security is sold prior to maturity.

These calculations and analysis allow banks to immunise their portfolios, meaning that the gains from a higher reinvestment rate are just offset by the capital loss. In the case of an individual security, a similar immunisation happens when an investor's holding period equals the duration of the security.

There are some limitations to duration gap analysis. For starters, it may be difficult to find assets and liabilities of the same duration to include in an institution's portfolio. Another limitation is that many accounts, such as deposit accounts, don't always have well defined cash flow patterns, which makes it difficult to calculate their duration. Finally, duration is affected not only by defaults by customers but also by prepayment—which can throw calculations off.

Basis Point Value

There are multiple ways to calculate the potential impact of risk. One such way is to use basis point value (BPV) which considers how much a position gains or loses for every 0.01% move in the yield curve for a particular product.[7]

A basis point is a unit of measure used to describe the percentage change in the value of the rate associated with a financial instrument, stocks, interest rates or bond yields—where it is most commonly used. One basis point is equal to 1/100th of a percentage point or 0.01%—or 0.0001 in decimal notation. When the US Federal Reserve raised interest rates by 25 basis points in December 2015, it basically raised them 0.25%.

BPV, in turn, considers the changes in the price of a bond or interest rates. It is a relatively easy way to understand a change in value involving small percentages, as is often the case with rates. It can be used to consider risk.

In the context of interest rates it is particularly useful to measure changes and differentials in rates and margins associated with those rates. BPV is more useful than percentage changes because these may be too small or unclear. Its greatest value is in the clarity it affords to the measurement of rates and changes in rates.

BPV can also be taken a step further to calculate or define the price value of a basis point (PVBP), which is the change in the value of a financial instrument given a change of one basis point. To calculate the PVBP simply take the initial price of an instrument and subtract the price if the yield changes by 1 BPV.

Immunisation and Hedging Interest Rate Risk

Two ways to minimise interest rate risk in the balance sheet of a bank or financial institution are immunisation and hedging. Banks immunise against interest rate risk by adjusting the duration of instruments in a portfolio to match the time horizon of each investment by

---

[7] For a more in-depth discussion of how BPV can be used to calculate risk, refer to the *Treasury Market Operations* volume in this series.

locking instruments at a fixed rate. A complete immunisation strategy using approaches such as cash flow matching, duration matching, volatility matching or convexity matching can also be known as arbitrage.

It can be difficult, however, to immunise a portfolio perfectly. An imperfect or incomplete immunisation strategy can be called hedging. Institutions also hedge interest rate risks through a variety of vehicles such as interest rate swaps, or by investing in vehicles that can balance the risks associated with other holdings.

Immunisation

Let's set aside banks and financial institutions for a moment and consider a bond portfolio that investors might hold. Investors may want to immunise portfolios against changes in interest rates and would do this by locking in a fixed rate of return for the amount of time they might want to hold the investment. Interest rates have a direct impact on bond prices, as rates go up bond prices go down and vice versa. However, if a bond portfolio is immunised, the investor receives a specific rate of return over a time period regardless of changes in rates. Granted, this can go two ways in terms of gains and losses. Rather, the portfolio is immunised against changes, in this case fluctuating interest rates. The easiest way to do this is for investors to set a target for returns and invest in products that would generate those returns, regardless of changes in interest rates.

The assumption behind immunisation is that yield curves are flat and that changes in interest rates result in parallel yield curves, either up or down so that:

$$R_t = A_t - L_t$$

where 'R' is the net cash flow at time 't', 'A' is the cash inflow and 'L' is the liabilities.

Although banks and financial institutions aim to be profitable, they also need to protect the value of the assets they hold in their balance sheets in the face of uncertainty, particularly uncertainty in regards to changes in interest rates. Immunisation techniques make it possible for institutions to limit exposure to fluctuations in rates. In the (very rare) event of a perfect immunisation strategy, an institution would face almost no risk from changes in interest rates. In effect, the aim of an immunisation strategy is to match the duration of assets and liabilities to minimise the impact of interest rates on the net worth of a bank.

Banks and financial institutions can immunise against movements in interest rates by ensuring that their overall balance sheets are not affected. This, in effect, means that the value and returns associated with assets move in exactly the opposite amount as liabilities in the event of a change in interest rates. There are several ways that banks can immunise their balance sheets including:

- **Cash flow matching:** The easiest form of immunisation, cash flow matching basically involves ensuring against a payout. For example, if a bank anticipates having to pay out HKD1,000 in 10 years, it could buy and hold a zero-coupon bond with a 10-year maturity and a redemption value of HKD1,000—in effect covering the output. The inflows would then exactly match the outflows over the time horizon and changes in interest rates would have no bearing on the bank's ability to cover its obligations.

A downside is that cash flow matching can be both difficult to do across hundreds of thousands of items and, ultimately, expensive.

- **Duration matching:** Easier to accomplish and infinitely more practical than cash flow matching is duration matching. This approach involves matching the duration of assets and liabilities. It is also possible, and indeed expected, to make the match profitable under changing interest rate conditions. In technical terms, it is possible to match the first interest rate derivatives of the price functions of assets and liabilities and make sure that the second derivative of the asset price function is greater than the second derivative of the liability price function.

- **Convexity matching:** Convexity describes the curvature of a yield curve. The idea behind this approach is to match the structure of assets and liabilities so that their convexity matches. It is typically used in conjunction with duration matching, as the two are interrelated.

- **Volatility matching:** Another approach is to match the impact of volatility in interest rates in the liabilities of a bank or financial institution with similar volatility in the assets—or in the outflows and inflows of cash that the bank may be responsible for.

Trading activities involving bond forwards, futures or options can also be used to immunise portfolios or entire balance sheets against movements in interest rates.

Hedging Interest Rate Risk

While immunisation is the best way to avoid interest rate risk, it is almost impossible to completely immunise the balance sheets of modern banks, which have extremely complex and diversified balance sheets. So institutions reach for the next tool in their toolbox to protect themselves against interest rate risk: hedging. Institutions hedge to protect their assets and liabilities against risks associated with movements in interest rates in either direction.

The BCBS says that banks should be both aware of, and have the capacity to manage, their risk exposures, such as the exposures caused by liquidity that arise from the use of foreign currency deposit and the extending of short-term credit lines. 'A bank should take account of the risks of sudden changes in foreign exchange rates or market liquidity, or both, which could sharply widen liquidity mismatches and alter the effectiveness of foreign exchange hedges and hedging strategies.'[8]

---

[8] Basel Committee on Banking Supervision: 'Principles for Sound Liquidity Risk Management and Supervision'. September 2008. p. 14.

Rarely are hedges perfect but they can help institutions to avoid volatility. Banks and financial institutions can use off-balance-sheet transactions to hedge their positions and protect against changes to interest rates. One way to hedge interest rate risk is to use interest rate swaps. Swaps make it possible to artificially hedge the interest rate sensitivity or duration of an asset or a liability.

Forward rate agreements, for example, allow one party to pay a fixed interest rate and receive payments against a floating one, with the payments calculated against a notional principal amount. Only the net payment is made, with the loser paying the winner. Institutions typically use forward rate agreements to hedge against a particular risk at a specific period in time.

Futures contracts can also be used to hedge against interest rate risk but this is less risky than a forward contract because it includes an intermediary.

Another useful hedging tool is a swap, which is basically an exchange. A swap is not unlike a combination of forward rate agreements as it involves institutions exchanging future cash flows—one institution might have a shorter time horizon in mind while the other might prefer to operate with a longer one. In a plain vanilla swap—the most common type—one side pays a fixed interest rate and receives a floating rate while the other side pays a floating rate and receives a fixed rate.

Finally, there are options—a contract for which the underlying security is a debt of some kind. Options are particularly useful to protect against floating-rate loans such as mortgages. There are different types of options such as embedded options (such as a bond with a call or put provision), caps (that include a ceiling and are, in effect, call options based on interest rates), floors (put options that are the mirror image of caps) and collars (which involve buying caps and floors simultaneously and can be used to lower the cost of hedging but may provide less benefits).

Net Interest Income Sensitivity Analysis

Net interest income refers to the revenue that banks generate from their assets—such as loans, mortgages and securities—minus the expenses associated with paying out liabilities such as deposits. The net interest income comes from the spread between the interest that banks pay out on their liabilities and the interest they earn on their assets. Different banks with different types of operations and balance sheets can have different levels of sensitivity to changes in interest rates. Banks with more variable rate assets or assets with longer maturity dates at fixed rates can have more sensitivity to changes in interest rates while others, with assets and liabilities that can be repriced more frequently, may have less sensitivity. Net interest income sensitivity analysis looks at the balance of these factors.

Risk to net interest income is inherent in the business of banking. Managing it properly is important to both the profitability of banks and the value that they generate for shareholders, says the BCBS. Financial institutions typically use multiple scenarios when analysing their net interest income sensitivity by projecting how their inflows and outflows of cash would react to different changes in interest rates. Under the most common scenarios, banks in Hong Kong typically take into consideration gradual changes to rates over a particular period of time, generally a year into the future. The assumptions used in net interest income sensitivity analysis are similar to those used in gap analysis, while also assuming that both assets and liabilities are reinvested in similar assets and liabilities as they come due.

One typical bank, for example, may consider increases or decreases in rates of up to 300 basis points, even when they may not reasonably expect rates to move by more than 200 basis points in the period in question. A typical analysis also considers that rates (at least in Hong Kong and most developed markets) rarely jump by 200 basis points in one shot but are more likely to move by, for example, 50 basis points a quarter over a period of a year.

Take, as an example, the balance sheet of a large Hong Kong bank for the year ending in 2012. That year, the bank earned HKD18,349 million in interest income and saw outflows of HKD6,052 in interest expenses. The net interest income was HKD12,297 million.[9] The question that net interest income sensitivity analysis aims to answer is how sensitive this income is to changes in interest rates. That year, the net interest income amounted to a little more than half the total operating income of the bank, so any changes could have a significant impact on operations.

As with gap analysis there are some limitations as to how accurate these estimates are. The most obvious of these is that the analysis is based on assumptions about future movements in interest rates, and these assumptions may or may not be accurate. And the assumptions go well beyond just the movement on rates to include loan and deposit growth rates that are derived from historical trends, economic forecasts and the outlook for the institution.

Securitisation

A final piece of the puzzle that banks regularly tackle when dealing with interest rate risk is securitisation, which involves taking a relatively illiquid asset and transforming it (or a group of many such assets) into securities that can be traded in an exchange or sold to investors. Mortgage backed securities, of the kind made infamous during the global financial crisis, are the best known among such securities. They are hardly the only one, though. Car loans and credit card loans can also be securitised. Banks and other institutions can use securitisation to deal with some of the interest rate risk associated with long-maturity assets that would otherwise generate little liquidity. The process has the added benefit of taking these instruments out of the balance sheet of banks and, in effect, reducing their capital requirements.

---

[9] From Standard Chartered Bank's consolidated income statement for the year ended 31 December 2012.

The BCBS published a revised securitisation framework in May 2015 to set out standards for regulatory capital requirements for securitisation exposures. The new framework aims to address an over-reliance on external ratings, low risk weights for highly-rated securitisation exposures, high risk weights for low-rated securitisation exposures, cliff effects and insufficient risk sensitivity. The new framework applies to both traditional and synthetic securitisations in the banking book. A traditional securitisation is a structure 'where cash flow from an underlying pool of exposures is used to service at least two different stratified risk positions or tranches reflecting different degrees of credit risk and where payments to the investors depend on the performance of the underlying exposures.' A synthetic securitisation is a structure 'with at least two different stratified risk positions or tranches that reflect different degrees of credit risk where the credit risk of an underlying pool of exposures is transferred, in whole or in part, through the use of funded or unfunded credit derivatives or guarantees that serve to hedge the credit risk of the portfolio and where the investors' potential risk is dependent on the performance of the underlying pool.'[10]

The securitisation process starts with a bank or other financial institution generating multiple mortgages or loans backed by actual property such as real estate or cars. All of those loans are grouped into a single pool that is then held in trust and acts as the collateral for the new security. The security can then be issued by a third-party, such as a large financial company or investment bank or even the same one that holds the original loans. The upshot is a new tradeable security backed by all those claims against the real property of the original borrowers. Adding to the complexity, the issuer can split the pool of loans into different tranches depending on the quality of the underlying asset and to match the risk tolerance of potential investors.

By allowing investors to buy shares in a large pool of assets, securitisation can generate liquidity. It can also help hedge against the interest rate risks associated with all those loans that have been bundled together.

The HKMA has been regulating asset securitisation, particularly in regards to mortgage backed securities (MBS). In some, but not all cases, securitised assets can be excluded from the balance sheet of a bank provided they qualify for a 50% risk weight. In 2014, the HKMA adopted a new set of standards issued by the BCBS.

The BCBS issued a revised securitisation framework in December 2014 as part of its Basel III reforms. The aim of the new reforms is to reduce reliance on external ratings to determine the quality of such securities while recalibrating risk weights for exposure to securitised assets. Banks with supervisory approvals can now use an internal ratings-based approach to develop models for credit risk as well as external ratings and a standardised approach based on formulas from regulators. In the wake of the GFC, however, when many MBS in the United States were backed by assets with inflated values, the BCBS has developed higher liquidity requirements for such assets.

---

[10]Basel Committee on Banking Supervision. 'BIS Revised Securitization framework'. Bank for International Settlements. May 14, 2015.

Summary

- Interest income represents a large portion of the total income of banks, often more than half. Movements in interest rates can have a definite impact on both the liquidity position and bottom line of a bank.

- Interest rate risk in the banking book (IRRBB) is a key component of the Basel capital framework. IRRBB 'refers to the current or prospective risk to the bank's capital and earnings arising from adverse movements in interest rates that affect the bank's banking book positions.' Too much IRRBB can threaten the capital base or the earnings of a bank or both.

- There are three main sub-types of IRRBB that BCBS identifies: gap risk, basis risk and option risk.

- Interest rate risk is generally divided into four categories that include: repricing or maturity mismatches from timing differences in rate changes and cash flow repricing; yield curve risk that reveals repricing mismatches; basis risk from imperfect correlations between rates of interest paid out and earned from different vehicles; and option risk associated with options included in bank assets and liabilities.

- Interest rate gap analysis measures risks generally associated with targets for net interest income and is a measure commonly used to assess both risks and liquidity. Gap analysis looks at the maturity and repricing schedules to generate indicators of the sensitivity of an institution's interest rate risk position and value to changes in interest rates.

- Gap analysis is limited in its scope. It relies on assumptions about future movements in interest rates and these assumptions themselves are based on estimations by management and may not necessarily reflect the market fully. Another limitation is that gap analysis may be affected by the link between rates and the value of foreign exchange, which it does not really address. An additional concern is that it does not really reflect other factors that may impact income, such as the mix of assets and liabilities in a bank's portfolio or market conditions that may affect deposits. Gap analysis also ignores the time value of money, overlooks zero-interest liabilities and does not take into account option risk.

- Duration analysis is an important factor in determining interest rate risk as it considers the amount of time that capital is committed to a particular investment product. Duration is the average time period of a capital commitment. The duration is also called the Macaulay duration. Duration analysis measures how sensitive a particular security is to changes in interest rates.

- The duration gap indicates the actual impact of changes in rates on the net worth of financial institutions. Measuring it and taking steps to minimise it can prevent significant negative impact from risk events.

- There are multiple ways to calculate the potential impact of risk. One such way is to use basis point value (BPV) which considers how much a position gains or loses for every 0.01% move in the yield curve for a particular product.

- Immunisation techniques allow institutions to limit exposure to fluctuations in interest rates. A perfect immunisation strategy would make it possible for an institution to face almost no risk from changes in interest rates. In effect, the aim of an immunisation strategy is to match the duration of assets and liabilities to minimise the impact of interest rates on the net worth of a bank.
- Institutions hedge to protect their assets and liabilities against risks associated with movements in interest rates in either direction.
- Net interest income refers to the revenue that banks generate from their assets such as loans, mortgages and securities—minus the expenses associated with paying out liabilities such as deposits. The net interest income comes from the spread between the interest that banks pay out on their liabilities and the interest they earn on their assets.
- Financial institutions typically use multiple scenarios when analysing their net interest income sensitivity by projecting how their inflows and outflows of cash would react to different changes in interest rates.
- Securitisation involves taking a relatively illiquid asset and transforming it (or a group of many such assets) into securities that can be traded in an exchange or sold to investors.

Key Terms

Assumptions	Interest rates
Basel Committee on Banking Supervision	Macaulay duration
Basis risk	Maturity
Duration analysis	Maturity mismatches
Duration gap	Mortgage-backed securities
Foreign exchange	Net interest income sensitivity analysis
Gap risk	Option risk
Hedging	Pricing risk
Immunisation	Reinvestment rate
Interest income	Repricing mismatches
Interest rate gap analysis	Risk
Interest rate risk	Securitisation
Interest rate risk in the banking book (IRRBB)	Yield curve risk

Review Questions

1. Describe and discuss the four different categories of interest rate risk. Why is interest rate risk an important consideration for banks?
2. Discuss the limitations of interest rate gap analysis. Why is such analysis useful? Why is it not always completely accurate?

3. Describe immunisation. What would a perfect immunisation strategy be like?
4. What is securitisation? What purpose does it serve for banks?

Further Reading

Basel Committee on Banking Supervision, 'Consultative Document: Interest rate risk in the banking book'. June 2015. http://www.bis.org/bcbs/publ/d319.pdf.

Basel Committee on Banking Supervision. 'Standards: Interest rate risk in the banking book'. Bank for International Settlements. April 2016.

Hong Kong Institute of Bankers (2014) *Treasury Markets and Operations*. Chichester: John Wiley & Sons.

Koch, Timothy W. and MacDonald, S. Scott (2010) *Bank Management*. Ohio, United States: South-Western Cengage Learning.

6

ALM in Changing Market Conditions

Learning outcomes

After studying this chapter, you should be able to:

1 Describe the causes and effects of the global financial crisis and some of the key lessons for regulators and banks.

2 Understand how stress tests work and be able to consider the factors necessary to design and implement an effective test.

3 Explain the links between stress testing and contingency planning.

4 Describe the impact of the interest rate cycle on the operations of a bank and how the cycle can impact asset and liability management strategy.

Introduction

As we have seen in previous chapters and in other books in this series, effective asset and liability management (ALM) is one of the most important activities of any profitable bank. Effective ALM is not static but dynamic. It does not take into account changes in market conditions but preempts them. Effective ALM planning includes planning, forecasting and anticipating. All options have to be considered and black swan events taken into account. History is replete with crises and failures caused by events that banks failed to anticipate or, worse, dismissed as unlikely.[1]

This chapter looks at how banks can use ALM to minimise the risk and the impact of risk events, both expected and unexpected. It is a natural conclusion to a book focused on ALM.

We'll first look at the global financial crisis (GFC). At the time of writing, the GFC is almost a decade old but its impact on the global economy is very much visible, from slower growth to an environment of pervasive low interest rates in the US and, by extension, in Hong Kong. The lessons learnt from the GFC have shaped the current regulatory environment for banks and led the Basel Committee on Banking Supervision (BCBS) to rework its capital adequacy rules.

From there, the chapter moves on to consider the link between stress testing and the execution of contingency plans. Stress tests have been in use for decades but the pressures of the GFC led to their growing importance. Regulators in North America, Europe and Asia are increasingly relying on stress tests to ensure that their banks are operating on solid capital footing, even in the face of significant adverse risk events.

The chapter then moves on to more practical implications and applications of all this planning, including the link between ALM strategy and the interest rate cycle. This is an important consideration. Changes in interest rates are a fact of life for banks. Reacting to these changes in a way that ensures ongoing profitability is key. To react effectively, however, banks must have plans in place that address both expected and unexpected changes.

It is not an exaggeration to say that effective ALM keeps banks alive. It is like food to a person, or rather, the planning that goes into ensuring a healthy three meals a day. A lack of such planning raises the risk of weakness and disease. It's the same with banks—a lack of effective ALM planning jeopardises the bank's future.

Lessons from the Global Financial Crisis

The lessons from the global financial crisis that started in 2007 were learned the hard way, and led to the restructuring of banks and their offerings. Almost a decade after the crisis,

---

[1] Kindleberger, Charles (2000) *Manias, Panics, and Crashes*. Hoboken, NJ: John Wiley & Sons.

regulators were still dealing with the fallout. The crisis started with a series of turbulences in financial markets between August 2007 and September 2008 which led to central banks stepping in with great pools of liquidity to cover the shaky balance sheets of banks. Then, on 15 September, 2008, Lehman Brothers announced its bankruptcy, which all but destroyed the credibility of the system not only in the United States but around the world. By the end of 2009, the crisis of confidence had moved across the Atlantic from the United States to the Euro area.

Before the crisis started, economies around the world had undergone an extended period of loose monetary policy, credit expansion and booms in asset prices. Much of Asia was, for its part, still recovering from the 1997 Asian financial crisis and the environment was one of sound macroeconomic fundamentals and well-capitalised banks but growing signs of financial exuberance. Through the end of 2007 and 2008, as central banks in the US and Europe entered into a period of aggressive policy easing, commodity prices spiked and inflation became the top concern for monetary authorities in Asia. By the end of 2008, as Lehman Brothers fell and the global financial system seized up, Asia was hit with heavy out-flows of capital, falling stock markets, a collapse in trade and easier monetary policy. What followed was a widespread contraction in GDP around the region and the announcement of large fiscal packages; while, elsewhere in the world, strong market interventions coin-cided with a recession in large economies in late 2008 and early 2009. It wasn't until the second quarter of 2009 that financial markets rallied and financial prospects improved in Asia while efforts in the West to strengthen the balance sheets of banks helped financial markets rally (see Figure 6.1).

The single most important lesson from the crisis, in the words of the former chairman of the US Federal Reserve Bank, Ben Bernanke, was the need for improved

FIGURE 6.1 The global financial crisis timeline

	Pre-crisis conditions	Phase 1	Phase 2	Phase 3	Phase 4
	(Before Q3 07)	(Q3 07–mid-Sep 08)	(mid-Sep 08–late 08)	(late 08–Q1 09)	(Q2 09–present)
Asia-Pacific	Sound macro fundamentals and banks; signs of financial exuberance	Inflation top policy concern; mild financial headwinds	Capital outflow; falling stock markets; trade collapse; much easier monetary policy	Sharp GDP contraction; large fiscal packages	Financial markets rally; green shoots; economic and financial prospects improve
World	Extended period of loose monetary policy, credit expansion and asset price booms	BNP funds suspended; aggressive policy easing; high commodity prices; liquidity support	Lehman Brothers bankruptcy; global finance freezes up; expanded liquidity support	Strong market interventions; synchronised G3 recession; fiscal stimulus	Steps to strengthen bank balance sheets; financial markets rally; G3 real activity still weak

Source: Filardo, Andrew et al. (2010) 'The international financial crisis: timeline, impact and policy responses in Asia and the Pacific.' *BIS Papers No 52.* http://www.bis.org/publ/bppdf/bispap52c.pdf.

supervision of the banking sector and the importance of using this supervision to strengthen capital, liquidity and risk management.[2] In Bernanke's words:

> Looking forward, I believe a more macroprudential approach to supervision—one that supplements the supervision of individual institutions to address risks to the financial system as a whole—could help to enhance overall financial stability. Our regulatory system must include the capacity to monitor, assess, and, if necessary, address potential systemic risks within the financial system.

Bernanke pointed to a few items that required tighter supervision including:

- Monitoring large or rapidly growing exposures across firms and entire markets, not just among individual institutions or sectors. A case in point was the growth of subprime mortgages in the US, the collapse of which led to the crisis.
- Better assessment of systemic risks implied in changing risk-management practices, widespread increases in leverage or changes to markets and products.
- Ongoing analysis of possible spillover effects among financial firms and markets, which includes the mutual exposures of firms that are very interconnected.
- Making sure that firms that are systemically important are adequately supervised, in a way that is commensurate with the risks that its failure would pose to the entire financial system.
- Developing a way to safely wind down systemically important institutions that are failing.
- Making sure that critical financial infrastructure is robust, including the institutions that support trading, payments, clearing and settlements.
- Mitigating pro-cyclical features of capital regulations as well as other rules and standards.
- Identifying regulatory gaps that could leave consumers and investors exposed and jeopardise the financial system.

Bernanke concluded: 'The events of the past two years have revealed weaknesses in both private-sector risk management and in the public sector's oversight of the financial system. It is imperative that we apply the lessons of this experience to strengthen our regulatory system, both at the level of its overall architecture and in its daily execution.'

Much has changed since that speech. The Basel Committee on Banking Supervision has introduced a series of reforms—most of which have been adopted by national regulators—with the aim of making banks and entire financial systems more resilient.

---

[2]Ben Bernanke made the comments during a speech at the Federal Reserve Bank of Chicago Conference on Bank Structure and Competition on 7 May, 2009: http://www.federalreserve.gov/newsevents/speech/bernanke20090507a.htm.

Different locations introduced different policies to deal with the aftermath of the crisis. Hong Kong dropped its base interest rate by a total of 3% between October 2008 and December 2008, but the Hong Kong Monetary Authority also changed the way it calculates its base rate, essentially setting it 0.5% higher than the FOMC's target range. Hong Kong also extended the maturity of borrowing from the HKMA's standing facility, started accepting USD assets as collateral and lowered the cost of borrowing from the HKMA while strengthening lender-of-last-resort operations. To provide more liquidity assistance, Hong Kong set up a swap line with mainland China of RMB22 billion in January 2009. The regulator also increased the coverage on bank deposits to HKD100,000, increased government guarantees on loans to small business and introduced a new Contingent Bank Capital Facility to make more capital available to banks. To limit short selling, penalties for failed settlements were doubled.[3]

For banks, perhaps the biggest lessons from the global financial crisis were the importance of being properly capitalised while having strong risk management strategies in place—risk management strategies that are regularly tested and backed by executable contingency plans. Compared to banks in other jurisdictions, Hong Kong banks sailed through the crisis with relative ease thanks to both their capital reserves and the very limited amount of sub-prime lending done in the market. Nevertheless, in the wake of the crisis, new and stronger standards were created to avoid such global-scale exposures in future.

One barrier to an appropriate level of capitalisation—one that became obvious during the GFC—has been the different notions of risk associated with the banking book and the trading book. Before the crisis, banks could put riskier assets in the trading book by claiming a 'trading intent'—a subjective concept, noted the BCBS in a paper in 2015.[4] The crisis exposed the fallacy of this approach, when instruments held in the trading book and not backed up by levels of reserves similar to those in the banking book generated billions in losses or pushed banks to shift illiquid positions into the banking book and subjecting them only to minimum capital requirements.

Banking book instruments are, in broad strokes, intended to be held to maturity, with changes in market value not reflected in financial accounts or capital account. The primary concern for these exposures has generally been default risk. Instruments held in the trading book are in a different position. The trading book is exposed to fair value losses through income associated with general movements in market rates and changes in credit spreads, while default risk remains a concern.

After the global financial crisis, the BCBS took the lead in reviewing the capital framework for market risk and to identify different capital treatment for similar types of risks across bank balance sheets.

---

[3] Filardo, Andrew et al. (2010) 'The international financial crisis: timeline, impact and policy responses in Asia and the Pacific.' *BIS Papers No 52*. http://www.bis.org/publ/bppdf/bispap52c.pdf.

[4] Basel Committee on Banking Supervision. 'Interest rate risk in the banking book'. Consultative Document. June 2015.

From Stress Testing to Contingency Plan Execution

The lessons from the global financial crisis were not lost on regulators around the world, virtually all of whom stepped up the rigour of the stress tests that they required banks to successfully complete. In the United States, the United Kingdom, across Europe and Asia—not least in Hong Kong—banks have long used stress tests to put their risk management and liquidity contingency plan through the fulcrum.

In theory, stress tests are relatively straightforward risk planning tools. They are an analysis or a simulation used to determine if a financial institution or a particular financial instrument can make it through a period of crisis. The idea behind stress tests is that institutions or regulators avoid estimating the potential impact of a risk event but rather work through the numbers to see what would happen in the event of, for example, a market crash of a certain size or the impact of a drop in economic growth into recession or a hike in interest rates. At their core, stress tests offer a type of scenario analysis that institutions and regulators can then use to determine the viability of specific products, entire institutions or even whole financial systems.

Stress testing requires the construction of credit risk models made up of a multiple regression model and a set of autoregressive models to examine the relationship between default rates of bank loans and various macroeconomic conditions. The stress tests allow regulators to assess the possible default rates of bank loans should a particular risk event come to pass. They also allow for a more precise calculation of value-at-risk (VaR).

Stress tests have become increasingly popular. The UK, for example, has a whole body of government—the Prudential Regulation Authority (PRA)—to carry out stress tests. The European Banking Authority (EBA) and the International Monetary Fund (IMF) also have entire departments dedicated to stress testing specific institutions with an eye on capital allocations and their ability to cover losses. At times, stress tests can lead to wholesale changes and more regulatory oversight, such as after 2014 when 25 banks failed stress tests carried out by the EBA.

Since 2013, the United States has shown a commitment to using stress tests and to following the standards set under Basel III. For regulators in the United States, the global financial crisis was a wake-up call. Up until 2007, banks carried out their own stress tests for internal purposes. It was not until after that year that regulators started requiring them. India, for example, passed legislation requiring them in 2007. The US started asking large banks to undergo stress tests twice a year starting in 2012 and, since 2014, mid-sized institution are required to undergo Dodd-Frank Act Stress Testing to quantify loan portfolio risk.

Stress tests are done by careful examination of the balance sheet of a particular institution. Some large banks started using internal stress tests in the early 1990s. The first iteration of the Basel Capital Accords in 1996 required banks to use stress tests to determine their ability to respond to market events.

Because the focus of stress tests is on few and specific risks, they are particularly useful as dry runs for contingency plans that banks should have in place to deal with specific risk events. Typically, stress tests focus on areas such as credit, market or liquidity risk, and depend on scenarios that the IMF describes as 'unlikely but plausible'. Banks—and any serious and large institution—should have in place contingency plans to deal with fires or earthquakes, two other unlikely but plausible risks. The same is true of the risks that stress tests are there to safeguard against.

The Basel III approach to stress testing is based on three different measures of capital adequacy based on loss distributions derived from historical data. The standardised approach uses risk weightings based on judgements by supervisors about the relative risk of different products and exposures. The internal ratings based (IRB) approach uses historical data to estimate level of losses that should be exceeded only once every 1,000 years. The advanced IRB approach uses a similar benchmark. There is an intrinsic irony that historical data is not always a good predictor of future risk. There is a wrinkle, however, in that stress tests should not be based on current balance sheet information but on future book capital under different scenarios along with estimates of losses in particular scenarios.[5]

The Hong Kong Monetary Authority (HKMA) is also increasingly reliant on stress tests to shore up the resilience of banks. The authority started putting more weight on those tests in 2014, when it warned of excessive credit growth and liquidity risk. Although banks in Hong Kong follow Basel III capital and liquidity requirements, they could still be vulnerable to the scenarios used for the stress tests. Unlike tests in previous years, the HKMA implemented a series of transparency policies and started working with banks to determine the indicators to be tested.

The HKMA puts some emphasis on contingency plans and the ability of banks to execute them. That is where access to sufficient liquidity comes into play. Contingency plans only work when the tools to implement them are accessible. After a series of stress tests in 2014, for example, the HKMA identified a dozen banks that needed to stabilise their capital bases—although the authority was quick to point out that these banks were local branches of foreign banks without a Hong Kong deposit base.

The HKMA has long had a framework in place to test the ability of banks in Hong Kong to withstand macroeconomic shocks, such as the Asian financial crisis, GFC or a hard landing in China. Over the years, the regulator has fine-tuned that framework to keep up with changes put forth by the BCBS, through Basel II and later Basel III. For example, in December 2014, the HKMA issued revisions to the securitisation framework to reduce a 'mechanistic reliance on external ratings, recalibrating risk weights for highly-rated and low-rated securitisation exposures, reducing cliff effects and enhancing risk sensitivity of the framework.' Scheduled to take effect in January 2018, the new framework applies to all

---

[5]Wall, Larry D. 'Basel III and Stress Tests'. Center for Financial Innovation and Stability. December 2013. Accessed online on 5 March 2016 at https://www.frbatlanta.org/cenfis/publications/notesfromthevault/1312.cfm.

securitisation exposures held in the banking book. It later followed up with a similar move for exposures in the trading book.[6]

In effect, the tighter framework creates closer links between stress testing and on-the-ground contingency planning by revising regulations in a number of areas. First is the hierarchy of approaches, putting an internal ratings-based approach at the top and requiring banks to obtain supervisory approval for internal credit risk models, followed by an external ratings-based approach and then a standardized approach. Only when none of these three approaches work can banks move on to using a risk-weighted exposure of 1,250%. A second areas of focus for the new framework is on the risk drivers used in each approach and the addition of additional ones, including a requirement to note the maturity of a securitisation tranche to minimise under-capitalisation. A third area of focus is on how the framework is calibrated, with capital requirements significantly increased and aligned with risks.

This framework, and its execution, provides one of multiple bridges available— between stress testing done to determine the ability of banks to withstand exposure, and the development of contingency plans that can help banks and the entire financial system navigate risk events. For regulators, the goal is to minimise any potential for market disruptions caused by risks by ensuring all institutions, not just those seen as systemically important, operate on a solid footing. For individual banks, the goal is similar, in that the transition from stress testing to contingency planning should be smooth and based on real risk assessments, rather than approaches that meet regulatory requirement without regard for actual market conditions.

ALM Strategy and Interest Rate Cycle

The ultimate aim of an effective asset and liability management (ALM) strategy is profitability within an acceptable level of risk to the bank. That is at the top of the ALM pyramid. This goal of profitability is supported on one side by regulatory compliance and, on the other, by effective risk management. A key risk to consider is interest rate risk.

An assets and liabilities management strategy must, to be effective, take into consideration the interest rate cycle. Important in this process is the identification of stress events for interest rate risk and credit spread risk, the application of strong modelling approaches and the appropriate and effective use of stress tests to develop contingency plans. This is a process with multiple stakeholders, including day-to-day managers in trading, treasury and finance departments, the Asset and Liability Management Committee (ALCO), the ALM team, risk managers and risk controllers and economists. All these different stakeholders

---

[6]Hong Kong Monetary Authority. 'Basel Capital Framework – Revisions to the Securitisation Framework'. B1/15C. 17 December 2014.

should come together to determine, in the words of the BCBS, 'the range of potential interest rate movements by currency over which it will measure exposure. Management should ensure that risk is measured over a reasonable range of potential rate change scenarios, including some containing severe stress elements.'

An effective strategy, by necessity, is based on stress tests that include severe and plausible scenarios. It makes little sense, for example, to focus stress tests on scenarios involving declines in market rates during times of low interest rates. In this regard, considering the interest rate cycle is of paramount importance. Banks and other financial institutions regularly use their ALM strategies to respond to changes in the market. Changes in interest rates are a key consideration. The good news is that, to a degree, changes in interest rates are predictable and usually expected. It is also possible to put in place contingency plans for any type of movement in interest rates.

To this end, ALM needs to be tied to the interest rate cycle of each and every market in which the bank or financial institution operates. Changes in interest rates can trigger inflows or outflows of capital, spur borrowing or depress it and impact customers' ability to service obligations as well as the costs and returns of the bank itself. Rising interest rates also, by necessity, can increase the credit risk of customers who are highly leveraged, and this is an important consideration for risk managers.

An effective approach to interest rate risk is dynamic and takes into consideration the ups and downs of business and interest rates. During recessionary times, interest rates tend to fall as regulators seek to encourage more borrowing, capital spending by businesses and more spending by individuals. During the recovery phase of the business cycle, the opposite is true. To curb inflation and keep growth within controllable levels, regulators typically raise interest rates (see Figure 6.2).

In the decade after the GFC, interest rates in the US, Europe, Japan and many other markets, including Hong Kong, were held at record low levels by regulators eager to spur growth. One boon for banks was the ease of planning that such predictability provided—at least in terms of interest rates. Change started slowly at the end of 2015, when the US Fed started cautiously raising rates. That move marked the beginning of a new cycle with an upwards trend.

FIGURE 6.2   Dynamic approach of ALM

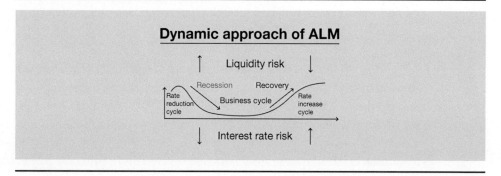

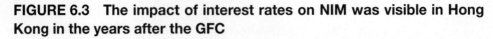

FIGURE 6.3   The impact of interest rates on NIM was visible in Hong Kong in the years after the GFC

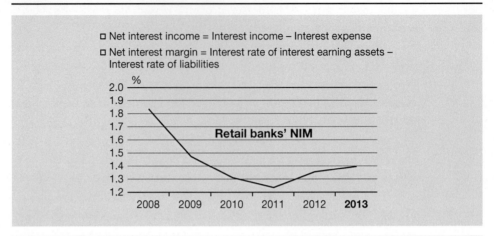

The interest rate cycle has a significant impact on ALM planning as it affects a range of products that make up both the assets and liabilities side of a bank's balance sheet. Bonds, and the returns that they generate, are impacted and so are the payments that banks have to make on them. Mortgages and loans are also affected, as a higher interest rate environment can cut down on the returns from long-term instruments with maturities of several years. On the assets side of the equation, net interest income (NII) is affected by changes in interest rates. On the liabilities side, net interest margin (NIM) is also impacted by changes in interest rates (see Figure 6.3).

Conventional lending such as retail and corporate loans with medium-term maturities are typically the largest asset category on the balance sheets of most banks. Their weight decreased somewhat after the GFC as a result of an erosion of NIM due to a deregulation of interest rates in Hong Kong and higher capital costs, with more banks moving to diversify their sources of income by boosting fee incomes and trading profits. Still, the ALM considerations associated with interest rates remain significant.

Another consideration is the impact of interest rates on the bond holdings of banks, holdings that have grown over time to support both investment banking and capital market businesses of most banks. A Basel III requirement that banks hold higher quantities of high quality liquid assets (HQLA) such as high grade bonds also led to the growth in bond holdings.

History provides far too many examples of the potentially catastrophic impact of ignoring interest rates. One famous such example is the Savings and Loan (S&L) Crisis through the 1980s in the US. At the end of the 1970s, the interest rate environment in the US became increasingly heated and led many investors to pull their funds from S&L institutions and put their money in money market funds. A big driver of this trend was Regulation Q , which put a cap on how much interest S&Ls could pay. Regulation Q was a

Federal Reserve Board rule enacted in accordance with the Glass-Steagall Act of 1933 to eliminate loan sharking.

Because these companies made most of their money from low-interest mortgages, they did not have the means to pay higher interest rates to depositors. Still, interest rates continued to rise. Eventually the government had to bail out a number of these institutions to the tune of US$124 billion while 747 of them were liquidated. S&L deposits were insured by the Federal Savings and Loan Insurance Corporation (FSLIC), which also became insolvent. It was not until the Dodd-Frank Act of 2010 that Regulation Q was, for all intents and purposes, repealed.[7]

The S&L Crisis, and its aftermath, is a prime example of the potentially devastating effect of large mismatches between ALM and movements in interest rates. The crisis was exacerbated by interest rate deregulation and the push by then Federal Reserve chairman, Paul Volcker, to raise benchmark rates. The rates that S&L could charge for their mortgages could not keep up with the rates that they had to pay for the funds to pay those mortgages. The S&L liability structure was short-term and based on floating rates but their asset structure was long-term, with many 30 years mortgages offered at fixed rate. All told, the asset losses added up to US$150 billion.

At the time of writing of this book in 2016, the interest rate cycle in the US is shifting from a long period of rates held at or near zero to slow but steady increases. This leads to important considerations for ALM and risk managers.

Rises in interest rates in the US could have multiple effects on Hong Kong banks. For starters, and this was seen during the last part of 2015, increases in interest rates in the US and the subsequent increase in yields that this leads to may trigger a reversal in portfolio investment away from emerging markets in Asia—investment that often flows through Hong Kong banks—increasing liquidity risk. The same reversal in the flow of investment could also increase funding costs, leading to interest rate risk. At the same time, a rise in interest rates in the US could make bond markets there more attractive while increasing market risk in Hong Kong and Asia through a decline of the bond markets.

On the other hand, rising interest rates in the US may create opportunities for banks in Hong Kong, particularly if other markets such as Europe remain in an environment of low rates. Such low rates could generate carry trade opportunities to borrow Euro at low rates and invest in HKD or RMB equities or bonds at much higher ones. At the same time, banks can use derivatives to reduce their Euro related currency risk.

It is the job of ALM to develop an appropriate strategy to deal with the interest rate cycle. This requires, to name a few examples, paying attention to deposits and potential deposit outflows or inflows, shifts in the mix of deposits and the amount of deposits held in interest bearing accounts, re-pricing of deposits and loans to minimise mismatches and the potential of a migration of retail deposits to money market funds (as interest rates rise).

---

[7] Barth, James R.; Trimbath, Susanne; Yago, Glenn (2004) *The Savings and Loan Crisis: Lessons from a Regulatory Failure*. Boston: The Milken Institute.

Summary

- The global financial crisis started in 2007 and led to the restructuring of banks around the world as well as many of their offerings. The crisis started with a series of turbulences in financial markets between August 2007 and September 2008 and on 15 September, 2008, Lehman Brothers announced its bankruptcy, which all but destroyed the credibility of the system not only in the United States but around the world.

- The single most important lesson from the crisis may have been the need for improved supervision of the banking sector and the importance of using this supervision to strengthen capital, liquidity and risk management.

- A number of areas require greater supervision including exposures across firms and entire markets; assessment of systemic risk and leverage as well as products; spillover effects from market changes; adequate levels of supervision; winding down of failing institutions; financial infrastructure; the pro-cyclical features of regulations; and regulatory gaps.

- For banks, perhaps the biggest lessons from the global financial crisis were the importance of being properly capitalised while having strong risk management strategies in place—risk management strategies that are regularly tested and backed by executable contingency plans.

- One barrier to an appropriate level of capitalisation—one that became obvious during the GFC—has been the different notions of risk associated with the banking book and the trading book. Banking book instruments are, in broad strokes, intended to be held to maturity, with changes in market value not reflected in financial accounts or capital account.

- Stress tests are an analysis or a simulation used to determine if a financial institution or a particular financial instrument can make it through a period of crisis. Stress tests allow regulators to assess the possible default rates of bank loans should a particular risk event come to pass. They also allow for a more precise calculation of value-at-risk (VaR).

- Stress tests are done by careful examination of the balance sheet of a particular institution.

- The HKMA has long had a framework in place to test the ability of banks in Hong Kong to withstand macroeconomic shocks, such as the Asian financial crisis, GFC or a hard landing in China. Over the years, the regulator has fine-tuned that framework to keep up with changes put forth by the BCBS, through Basel II and later Basel III.

- The ultimate aim of an asset and liability management (ALM) strategy is profitability.

- Banks and other financial institutions regularly use their ALM strategies to respond to changes in the market. Changes in interest rates are a key consideration.

- An effective approach to interest rate risk is dynamic and takes into consideration the ups and downs of business and interest rates.

- The interest rate cycle has a significant impact on ALM planning as it affects a range of products that make up both the assets and liabilities side of a bank's balance sheet.
- On the assets side of the equation, net interest income (NII) is affected by changes in interest rates. On the liabilities side, net interest margin (NIM) is also impacted by changes in interest rates.
- The Savings and Loan Crisis in the 1980s in the US is a famous example of how a mismatch in interest rates can lead to systemic levels of defaults. Eventually the government had to bail out a number of these institutions to the tune of US$124 billion while 747 of them were liquidated.
- Rises in interest rates in the US could have multiple effects on Hong Kong banks.

Key Terms

Asian Financial Crisis (AFC)

Asset and liability management (ALM)

Banking book

Basel Committee on Banking Supervision (BCBS)

Basel III

Ben Bernanke

Bonds

Capitalisation

Contingency planning

Credit risk

Credit risk models

Exposures

Glass-Steagall Act

Global Financial Crisis (GFC)

Hong Kong Monetary Authority (HKMA)

Interest rate cycle

Interest rate risk

Interest rates

Lehman Brothers

Money market funds

Net interest income (NII)

Net interest margin (NIM)

Regulation Q

Risk management

Savings and loan (S&L) crisis

Stress tests

Systemic risk

Trading book

US Federal Reserve Bank

Value-at-risk (VaR)

Review Questions

1. Describe the events that led to the global financial crisis. How did regulators react? What was the aftermath?
2. What are stress tests? What is their aim? Describe the main elements of an effective stress test.

3. How can changes in interest rates affect the asset and liability management plans of a bank?
4. Describe the current trend in interest rates in your market. At which stage of the cycle are rates?

Further Reading

Barth, James R.; Trimbath, Susanne; Yago, Glenn (2004) *The Savings and Loan Crisis: Lessons from a Regulatory Failure*. Boston: The Milken Institute.

Basel Committee on Banking Supervision. 'Interest rate risk in the banking book'. Consultative Document. June 2015.

Filardo, Andrew et al. (2010) 'The international financial crisis: timeline, impact and policy responses in Asia and the Pacific.' *BIS Papers No 52*. http://www.bis.org/publ/bppdf/bispap52c.pdf.

Kindleberger, Charles (2000) *Manias, Panics, and Crashes*. Hoboken, NJ: John Wiley & Sons.

Wall, Larry D. 'Basel III and Stress Tests'. Center for Financial Innovation and Stability. December 2013. Accessed online on 5 March 2016 at https://www.frbatlanta.org/cenfis/publications/notesfromthevault/1312.cfm.

7

Case Studies

Learning outcomes

After studying this chapter, you should be able to:

1 Identify and evaluate how market factors impact the profitability of banks in light of specific case studies.

2 Compare and select different approaches of bank asset and liability management and evaluate the appropriateness of the strategies adopted by the Royal Bank of Scotland, Lehman Brothers, Continental Illinois National Bank and the Bank of New England to fulfill their objectives.

3 Demonstrate how market risks and liquidity risks overlapped to exert pressure on the capital of Royal Bank of Scotland, Lehman Brothers, Continental Illinois National Bank and the Bank of New England and identify strategic considerations in capital planning.

4 Identify how interest rate risks threatened the stability of financial institutions and critically evaluate how effective the technical strategies adopted by Royal Bank of Scotland, Lehman Brothers, Continental Illinois National Bank and the Bank of New England were in immunizing institutions against such risks.

Introduction

The discussion of how banks undertake their assets and liabilities management that we have undertaken so far has been mostly theoretical, albeit with a solid grounding in practical experience. This chapter takes those discussions into the realm of real life and the actual and devastating impact that improper ALM can have on bank operations.

The aim of the case studies in this chapter is to examine and analyse the sequence of events that led to a pair of famous management failures. We will first look at the timing of events and the manner in which various indicators of bank condition reflected growing problems. These case studies are examples of how a combination of inadequately managed BALM have brought down both global and domestic banks. Their misfortunates are invaluable lessons learnt and stand in sharp contrast with the famous 17 fundamental principles for the management and supervision of liquidity risk. Together they can be considered the 'Do and Don't in BALM' to bring the journey of this book to a close. Successful BALM is a tricky balancing act—to get the right tradeoff between maximising profit, staying liquid and achieving sustainable growth. It is also about maintaining the right attitude—not being complacent and staying vigilant all the time. We expect BALM will increasingly become a high priority for banks. History has indicated even the most powerful central bank on Earth cannot preempt the GFC.

The first case study looks at Royal Bank of Scotland and its failure, in 2016, of stress testing done by the Bank of England. The failure highlighted a series of chronic weaknesses in the bank's balance sheet that could be traced back to a time before the global financial crisis of 2007 and the subsequent government bailout of the bank. At the time of the tests, the UK government still owned more than 70% of the historied RBS.

The second case study examines the failure of Lehman Brothers, the venerable US bank that would fall down in the most spectacular banking failure to date. Lehman, which could trace its history to 1850, went bankrupt during the sub-prime crisis in the US in 2008, not long after reporting its most profitable year ever. Ultimately, the collapse was caused by large positions in low-rated mortgage tranches that the company had taken when securitising underlying mortgages. In 2006, Lehman securitised US$146 billion in mortgages. In 2007 the bank reported net income of US$4.2 billion but had a mortgage-backed securities portfolio of $85 billion. When the housing market in the US burst, the mismatches between Lehman's assets and liabilities became exposed. The following year, the bank went bankrupt.

The third case study focuses on the events that led to the fall of Continental Illinois Bank, which faced a liquidity crisis of major proportions in the late 1980s. Until the seizure of Washington Mutual in 2008, the bailout of Continental represented that largest bank failure in US history. In fact, the sheer size of the bank, the seventh largest in the United States with US$40 billion in assets at the time, necessitated the giant bailout. The consequences of a bankruptcy of such a large entity would have been too far reaching to contemplate. The events at Continental Illinois have come to be known as the prime modern example of systemic risk in modern banking history. The events that unfolded hold lessons for asset and liability managers, risk managers and regulators. Even now, some three decades after those difficult events, the resolution that came to be known as the 'Continental divide' has emerged as the prototype for numerous bank restructurings around the world.

A fourth case study examines the impact on the Bank of New England Corp. in Massachusetts, United States, of virtually unchecked lending, particularly in real estate, through the 1980s. When the real estate market in the area began to falter in 1990 after years of rapid growth, the problems for the bank started. By the beginning of 1991 the bank and two sister institutions failed.

These case studies are telling examples of the challenges that both regulators and the banks themselves face when dealing with risk within financial institutions that take excessive amounts of risks even when their performance is in no way compromised.

Liquidity Risk: Royal Bank of Scotland Fails Stress Test (2016)

At the end of 2016, one of the most recognisable names in banking in the United Kingdom faced a significant hurdle when it failed a mandatory stress test. Edinburgh-based Royal Bank of Scotland (RBS) faced a choice: raise GBP2bn in capital or face a risk crisis. The discovery proved to be a significant problem for the government of the UK, which controlled 72% of the bank at the time. RBS was not the only bank to fail the most rigorous stress test to date by the Bank of England (BoE)—both Barclays and Standard Chartered also failed—but none as dramatically as RBS. Both Lloyds Banking Group and HSBC passed the test, as did Nationwide and Santander UK. As one banking chief executive told the *Financial Times*: 'It is staggering they are still failing, we all know how much capital we need.'

Almost three centuries old, RBS was one of the largest financial organisations in the world before the global financial crisis (GFC)—if not the 'largest bank in the world', as many called it. In 2007, it had 35 million customers in 30 countries served by 135,000 employees that worked in 4,500 business units. It reported income of GBP28bn and profits of GBP9.4bn on assets of GBP871bn. At its peak, it was the second largest bank in Europe and the tenth largest company in the world.

Between 2006 and 2008, CEO Sir Fred Goodwin let loose the Global Banking & Markets (GBM) and UK Corporate Banking arms and they grew their assets from GBP500bn to GBP830bn by 2008. GBM made up about half of the group's risk-weighted assets, according to an investigation by the *Daily Telegraph*.[1] As bank executives explained

---

[1]Wilson, H., Aldrick, P. and Ahmed K. (2011) 'Royal Bank of Scotland investigation: the full story of how the "world's biggest bank" went bust'. *The Telegraph*. Accessed online at http://www.telegraph.co.uk/finance/newsbysector/banksandfinance/8496654/Royal-Bank-of-Scotland-investigation-the-full-story-of-how-the-worlds-biggest-bank-went-bust.html.

to the newspaper, the atmosphere in the global banking environment in 2007 was one that demanded almost constant growth. The RBS group had total assets of GBP870bn at the end of 2006 but that skyrocketed to GBP1.9trn a year later after the controversial acquisition of the giant Dutch bank ABN. By the end of 2008, it emerged that the GBM arm's balance sheet had exploded to GBP1.2trn with 100-times leverage.

But then, at the end of 2008, RBS almost went bust, a casualty of the GFC and too much exposure to mortgage-backed securities that were at the epicentre of the global melt-down. An investigation by the Financial Services Authority (FSA) of the UK found no regulatory fault, simply bad decisions.

Some eight years after the GFC, some banks in the United Kingdom were still struggling to manage their assets and liabilities in a way that would raise their capital adequacy to levels high enough to satisfy regulators. Few banks, however, had as many issues as RBS, which had to be bailed out to the tune of GBP45bn to survive the GFC and spent close to a decade shedding non-performing or loss-making assets while rebuilding its financial strength. Despite years of efforts, RBS still failed a rigorous stress test at the end of 2016. When the Bank of England (BoE) set out to test the resilience of the biggest banks in the country, it found that RBS needed to find another GBP2bn to survive its stress scenarios.[2]

The test 'applied a hypothetical adverse scenario to the Group's balance sheet as at 31 December 2015 and compared the theoretical Common Equity Tier 1 ("CET1") ratio and Tier 1 leverage ratio positions of RBS before and after the impact of strategic management actions', the bank explained in a statement. These strategic actions included CRD IV distribution restrictions and the conversion of more Tier 1 securities. According to the results of the stress test, the bank's CET1 ratio, under the hypothetical scenario, would have been 5.5%, below the 6.6% requirement of the Individual Capital Guidance of the BoE and well below the 7.1% requirement after the CET1 Systemic Reference Point requirements. Even after the hypothetical conversion of some securities, the bank's ratio would still have fallen short of the Systemic Reference Point requirements. One percentage point of the CET1 ratio was equivalent to around GBP750m.[3]

The problems at RBS were myriad. One issue was the cost of litigation, which ate away at the bank's bottom line. The bank also had to deal with a series of costs associated with historical misconduct, impaired assets and noncore assets. The bank was also still dealing with fines from US authorities that some expected to add up to more than USD12bn misrepresenting mortgage securities before the GFC.

---

[2]Arnold, M. & Binham, C. (1 December, 2016) 'RBS emerges as biggest failure in tough UK bank stress tests'. *Financial Times*. Accessed online at: https://www.ft.com/content/85bab29e-b6ca-11e6-961e-a1acd97f622d?accessToken=zwAAAVujwidwkdOFurKetsoR5tOWHqGs2X9iLQ.MEYCIQDUalpuPi-fewijL4TYmTgsSk-0eSImL-gR-P-EUlv1IAIhAOOoaxwlkD5s58Xvh8JiQvDKcN1E8GhovDSi_u091hCL&sharetype=gift.

[3]Royal Bank of Scotland. (2016, Nov. 30) Statement on the publication of the 2016 Bank of England stress test results. Accessed online at: http://otp.investis.com/clients/uk/rbs/RNS/regulatory-story.aspx?cid=365&newsid=822893.

While the stress test was a comprehensive exercise, the bottom line result for RBS was that, as of the end of 2015, its Tier 1 capital ratio, which is a key indicator of financial strength, would have dropped by 10% in a stress scenario to just 5.5% before any actions by management could take effect. More troubling, even after management interventions and the sale of bonds in place specifically to be converted into equity in the event of a crisis, RBS would still have fallen short of the required reference point. In the words of the BoE: 'The stress test demonstrates that RBS remains susceptible to financial and economic stress.'

Chronology

The RBS stress test failure was an event that evolved over time.

- **1727:** Royal Bank of Scotland founded in Edinburgh, Scotland.
- **1960:** RBS opens first international office in New York.
- **1988:** RBS buys Citizens Financial Group, in Rhode Island, US.
- **2000 (11 Feb):** RBS wins bid to take over National Westminster Bank (Natwest), making it the second largest bank in the UK after HSBC.
- **2001:** Sir Fred Goodwin becomes CEO of RBS.
- **2004:** RBS acquires Charter One Bank and becomes the eighth largest bank in the US.
- **2005:** RBS expands into China with 10% stake in Bank of China acquired for GBP1.7bn.
- **2005:** New international HQ opens at Gogarburn, outside Edinburgh.
- **2005:** RBS wins Wharton Infosys Business Transformation Award for using technology in a way that transforms society.
- **2007:** RBS leads a consortium to acquire the large Dutch bank ABN AMRO, along with Spanish bank Santander and Belgian lender Fortis.
- **2007:** RBS has about GBP6bn in exposure to collateralised debt obligations (CDOs), with subprime making up GBP4.5bn.
- **2007 (9 Aug):** Credit crunch begins when BNP Paribas shuts down several hedge funds.
- **2007 (Sept):** First run on a British bank in 150 years begins. Newcastle-based Northern Rock has to seek emergency funds from BoE.
- **2008 (Apr):** RBS announces GBP12bn rights issue, the largest cash call to date in Britain's equity market.
- **2008 (9 June):** Capital raising closes but RBS market capitalisation down by a quarter, a loss greater than the latest round of fund raising.
- **2008 (28 Sept):** Fortis is nationalised. Authorities from the Netherlands, Belgium and Luxemburg pump in EUR11.2bn. Fortis is forced to sell its stake in the acquisition vehicle for ABN. The entire acquisition now falls on RBS.
- **2008 (7 Oct):** RBS in middle of virtual run by corporate customers. RBS shares crash 20%. BoE realises RBS does not have enough capital to survive. The BoE starts providing emergency liquidity assistance.

- **2008 (8 Oct):** Plan announced for Abbey, Barclays, HBOS, HSBC, Lloyds TSB, Nationwide, RBS and Standard Chartered banks to commit to increasing total tier 1 capital by GBP25bn. The Treasury then makes available another GBP25bn. The government also boosts significantly its Special Liquidity Scheme to GBP200bn and, with other measures, makes available GBP450bn in funding support.
- **2008 (12 Oct):** Over the weekend, Sir Fred Goodwin is forced to step down. Stephen Hester appointed CEO.
- **2008:** UK government uses taxpayer funds to pour GBP45bn into RBS and takes a 78.3% stake in the bank.
- **2010 (2 Dec):** Financial Services Authority (FSA) of the UK closes its investigation into the collapse of RBS.
- **2012 (23 Oct):** RBS agrees to pay USD42.5m to the state of the Nevada, US, to settle fines associated to links with mortgage lenders.
- **2013 (Mar):** BoE Financial Policy Committee (FPC) recommends regular stress tests of UK banking system to assess the capital adequacy of the system.
- **2013 (3 May):** RBS announces plan to sell assets, including Citizens Financial Group, while posting first quarterly profit since 2011.
- **2013 (1 Oct):** Ross McEwan appointed CEO of RBS.
- **2013 (11 Dec):** RBS pays USD100m in fines to New York and federal banking regulators in the US to settle civil investigations of concealing transactions with customers from countries facing sanctions.
- **2015 (Feb):** RBS reports seventh consecutive annual loss.
- **2015 (Oct):** BoE publishes its approach to stress testing the UK banking system.[4]
- **2015 (30 Oct):** RBS sells last remaining stake in Citizens Bank, raising USD2.6bn in total.
- **2015 (31 Dec):** Date BoE uses to carry out its stress test.
- **2016 (30 Nov):** BoE announces RBS must find GBP2bn after failing stress test. The bank's shares fall 1.2%.
- **2016 (1 Dec):** BoE approves RBS's new capital plan overnight.
- **2017 (27 Mar):** BoE publishes updated stress test scenarios for 2017.

Response and Management

The RBS failure of the BoE's most stringent stress tests to date represented the second largest percentage fall in capital under a stressed scenario since the test was implemented. In 2014, Co-operative Bank had suffered a large fall. Immediately after the failure, RBS submitted a revised capital plan that included 'further decreasing the cost base of the bank'

---

[4]Bank of England. Stress Test. http://www.bankofengland.co.uk/financialstability/Pages/fpc/stresstest.aspx.

while cutting risk-weighted assets and noncore loans and loan portfolios, the bank said in a statement.

After years spent in virtually constant crisis mode, RBS was well versed in crisis communication and response. In this case, the bank's response was immediate and well-coordinated. The bank's first statement came out hours after the BoE's announcement and the plan that was put in place seemed effective. It is worth noting, however, that the problem RBS faced was not one of public relations but of BALM, and that important response was in that arena.

The BoE picked 31 December, 2015, as the date for its stress test—meaning it relied on the bank's balance sheet as of that date. Since then, however, the bank has taken several steps to shore up its capital adequacy and resilience.

For starters, it ran down its risk-weighted assets by 21% or GBP10.4bn to GBP38.6bn in the first nine months of 2016. It also reduced higher risk credit portfolios, settled court cases and dealt with investigations by regulators. It also issued GBP2bn in securities. The result of all these actions was that the bank's CET1 ratio under normal circumstances was 15% as of the third quarter of 2016, higher than the bank's own target of 13% but lower than the 15.5% ratio recorded at the end of 2015. Significantly, however, that lowered ratio should have been more resilient through the elimination of risky assets.

Almost immediately after the results were announced, the bank agreed on a revised capital plan with the BoE to improve its resilience to stress conditions 'in light of the various challenges and uncertainties facing both the bank and the wider economy'. The bank announced plans to cut costs and further reduce its exposure to risky assets. RBS announced further costs cuts, including job reductions.

CEO Ross McEwan, who planned to bring the bank back to both profitability and private ownership, led the bank through a number of asset disposals, including the sale of Citizens Financial Group in the US which generated USD2.6bn for RBS. Unfortunately, just as he started to consider the possibility of reinstating dividends and was eyeing a possible first profitable year for the bank after seven years of losses, he had to deal with the setback created by the failure of the stress test. The setback did not compare to the crisis of the GFC but it did spur the CEO to announced further plans to shrink the bank and cut costs through 2017. In broad strokes, however, RBS's new plan was generally well received by regulators.

Analysis

One key goal of effective ALM is to ensure capital adequacy for banks, in other words, to make sure there is a match between the assets and liabilities of the bank so that a bank always has access to enough capital to cover its liabilities. Mismatches can be caused by problems on either side of the balance sheet. A ballooning of costs following risk events, foreseen or otherwise, can wreak havoc with a bank's ALM. Market crashes, such as the GFC, combined with heavy fines came together in the case of RBS to bring the bank to its knees. And then the UK government stepped in with a giant bailout.

RBS had grown too big to let fail, as far as the government of the UK was concerned. In the years leading up to the GFC, RBS grew rapidly—not unlike many other of the largest banks in the world. Unfortunately, its capital adequacy did not follow suit. Between 2005 and 2009, the bank's total assets more than doubled from GBP777m to GBP1.7bn while its risk weighted capital rose from GBP371m to GBP541m. In a decade, RBS had built a massive balance sheet worth GBP2.2trn—double the size of the Scottish economy.

The giant injection of cash from the UK government was not the end of the troubles for RBS but, rather, the beginning of a very long solution. The cash kept the bank afloat but it did not protect it from future crashes. Even as the injection of capital went into the bank's balance sheet, bank regulators were working on new adequacy standards in the wake of the GFC that required different types of liquidity reserves and more of them. Additionally, RBS not only had to cover its liabilities but it also had to shore up its capital reserves while eliminating loss-making operations and dealing with mismatches in assets and liabilities as well as legacy issues, not the least of which were significant non-performing assets and regulatory risk in the form of unpredictable fines in the US that could run into the billions. Table 7.1 lays out how this played out in practical terms.

In the decade that followed the bailout from the UK government, RBS reduced its giant footprint. No longer the 'largest bank in the world' it did manage to return, if not to profitability, to stability, all the while operating under a regulatory microscope. A problem that remained, however, was regulatory risk. Close to a decade after the GFC, RBS still faced billions of dollars in fines from a probe in the US into mortgage-backed securities. Those fines, the size of which was somewhat unpredictable, weighed on the bank as did rising loan impairments through 2015 and losses from the sale of a business— Williams & Glyn—which was nevertheless a necessary step to bringing the bank back to profitability.

Still, now under government ownership, RBS had to find a way to meet its capital adequacy requirements. Taxpayer funds kept it afloat until markets stabilised. A decade later, the bank certainly found itself on more solid footing but it was still coming up short of the capital adequacy requirements required by regulators. Years after the GFC and the hubris that led to the bank's massive expansion in the first decade of the century, RBS was still dealing with legacy issues.

RBS had come incredibly close to bringing down the UK's banking system once and remained, in the words of one analyst, the 'weak link in the UK banking chain'.[5]

---

[5]Treanor, J. (2016) 'RBS fails Bank of England stress test'. *The Guardian*. Accessed online at https://www.theguardian.com/business/2016/nov/30/rbs-fails-bank-of-england-stress-test.

TABLE 7.1   RBS projected consolidated solvency ratios in the stress scenario

	Actual (end-2015)	Minimum stressed ratio (*before the impact, of 'strategic' management actions or AT1 conversion*)	Minimum stressed ratio after 'strategic' management actions and before conversion of AT1		Minimum stressed ratio (*after the impact of 'strategic' management actions and conversion of AT1*)	Hurdle rate	Systematic reference point	Actual (2016 Q3)	Submit revised capital plan?
			Non-dividend 'strategic' management actions only(i)	All 'strategic' management actions including CRD IV distribution restrictions					
Common equity Tier 1 ratio(a) (b)	15.5%	5.5%	5.8%	5.9%	6.7%	6.6%(j)	7.1%	15.0%	Revised capital plan received and accepted
Tier 1 capital ratio(c)	19.1%	8.1%(f)	8.5%(f)	8.5%(f)	8.5%(f)			19.1%	
Total capital ratio(d)	24.7%	12.5%(f)	12.8%(f)	12.9%(f)	12.9%(f)			24.1%	
Memo: risk weighted assets (£ billion)	243	255(f)	255(f)	255(f)	255(f)			235	
Memo: CET1 (£ billion)	37.6	14(f)	15(f)	15(f)	17(f)			35.2	
Tier 1 leverage ratio(a)(e)	5.6%	2.7%	2.9%	2.9%	2.9%	3.0%	3.2%	5.6%	
Memo: leverage exposure (£ billion)	702(g)	591(h)	591(h)	591(h)	591(h)			703	

a The low points for the common equity Tier 1 (CET1) ratio and leverage ratio shown in the table do not necessarily occur in the same year of the stress scenario and correspond to the year where the minimum stressed ratio is calculated after all 'strategic' management actions and before conversion of AT1.

b The CET1 ratio is defined as CET1 capital expressed as a percentage of risk-weighted assets (RWAs) where CET1 capital is defined in line with the UK implementation of CRD IV as set out in the PRA Rulebook and relevant Supervisory Statements in *Supervisory Statement SS7/13*, 'CRD IV and capital', December 2013, and RWAs are defined in line with the UK implementation of CRD IV as set out in the PRA Rulebook and relevant Supervisory Statements, December 2013.

c Tier 1 capital ratio is defined as Tier 1 capital expressed as a percentage of RWAs where Tier 1 capital is defined as the sum of CET1 capital and additional Tier 1 capital in line with the UK implementation of CRD IV.

d Total capital ratio is defined as total capital expressed as a percentage of RWAs where total capital is defined as the sum of Tier 1 capital and Tier 2 capital in line with the UK implementation of CRD IV.

e The leverage ratio is calculated in line with the Policy Statement 'The Financial Policy Committee's powers over leverage ratio tools', July 2015.

f Corresponds to the same year as the minimum CET1 ratio over the stress scenario.

g Leverage exposure measure taken from the bank's annual accounts.

h Corresponds to the same year as the minimum leverage ratio over its stress scenario.

i This includes CRD IV distribution restrictions. Where a bank is subject to such restrictions all non business as usual cuts to distributions subject to CRD IV restrictions will appear in the next column – 'All 'strategic' management actions including CRD IV distribution restrictions'. This should not be interpreted as a judgement by the Bank that any or all of such cuts are conditional on such restrictions.

j The hurdle rate for CET1 ratios refers to the Individual Capital Guidance.

Source: RBS

Lessons Learnt

A number of key lessons emerged from the stress test failure at RBS:

- The process of effective ALM is made that much more complicated when there are thousands of units operating independently and with little transparency or thorough understanding by the board.
- Regaining financial strength after a crisis of the order of magnitude of the GFC requires a significant reassessment of a bank's balance sheet.
- Regulatory risk can be significant and put a bank's balance sheet in jeopardy.
- BALM can only be effective if it takes into account all types of risk, including both market risk and regulatory risk. To effectively manage risk, banks need to ensure they meet capital adequacy ratios.

Liquidity Risk: Lehman Brothers (2008)

The bankruptcy filing of Lehman Brothers Holdings Inc. was the largest in the history of the United States and perhaps the greatest failure of BALM management to date. The impact of the failure was felt around the world and lessons learnt have been hardwired into the global financial system.[6]

Lehman Brothers started out as a grocery store opened by Henry Lehman, a German immigrant, in Alabama, US, in 1850. The business expanded enormously over more than a century and a half. It survived railroad bankruptcies, the Great Depression, two world wars and a merger and a spin-off from American Express to become the fourth largest investment bank in the United States. In 2007, it celebrated its largest profit ever. In 2008, it went bankrupt.

Lehman did not survive the subprime mortgage crisis in the US in 2008. Rather, poor ALM and weak risk controls brought down the once-celebrated bank. Ultimately, the collapse was caused by large positions in subprime and other lower-rated mortgage tranches that the company had taken when securitising underlying mortgages. In 2006, Lehman securitised US$146 billion in mortgages. The year 2007 was a golden one for the company. It reported record net income of US$4.2 billion even as it accumulated a mortgage-backed securities portfolio of $85 billion. Even after the housing market in the US started to fray, Lehman held on to its enormous mortgage positions. The company did not budge when defaults on subprime mortgages rose to seven-year highs at the beginning of 2007.

---

[6]Adapted from *Treasury Management Operations*—another book in this series.

The first signs of trouble at Lehman surfaced on March 16, 2008. JP Morgan Chase acquired Lehman's rival in underwriting mortgage-backed securities, Bear Stearns, through a stock swap that valued that once lofty bank at $2 per share. The sale, or rescue, of Bear Stearns was a watershed moment in the global financial crisis. It was not long before speculation spread that Lehman could become the next Bear Stearns, even as most observers thought Lehman was simply too big to follow the same path.

In a single day, on March 17, Lehman's stock fell as much as 48 per cent and it kept on dropping. The valuation of Lehman's huge mortgage portfolio was questioned even when things seemed to look up when the company raised US$4 billion through an issue of preferred stock that was convertible into Lehman shares at a 32 per cent premium to its price at the time.

But, in June 2008, Lehman reported its first quarterly loss in the 14 years since it had become independent of American Express. The company lost $2.8 billion but managed to raise $6 billion from investors as one of the many measures to reverse the slide in its share value and its future prospects. Lehman said it had boosted its liquidity pool to an estimated US$45 billion, decreased gross assets by US$147 billion and reduced its exposure to residential and commercial mortgages by 20% while cutting down leverage from a factor of 32 to about 25. This Herculean effort was not enough.

Lehman's stock plunged 77 per cent in the first week of September 2008 and continued falling the next week. It lost 45% on 9 September, dropping to US$7.79. Its prospects became even murkier when the Korea Development Bank backed out of a plan to buy the once-venerable institutions for US$4 billion, a fraction of what it was once worth. And then Lehman's clients started pulling out—quickly. For the third quarter of 2008, Lehman reported losses of US$3.9 billion. The business was hemorrhaging capital. On 11 September, 2008, Lehman's stock plunged again, this time by 42%. Last ditch efforts to arrange for a takeover of the ailing investment bank by Barclays plc and Bank of America were fruitless.

Lehman Brothers filed for bankruptcy with the United States Bankruptcy Court for the Southern District of New York on 15 September, 2008. That day, the company's stock price hit a rock bottom 21 cents per share. The failure of Lehman marked the beginning of the global financial crisis that would last until 2012 and emerge as the worst financial crisis since the 1930s.

Chronology

The failure of Lehman Brothers evolved over several years.

- **1850:** Henry, Emanuel and Mayer Lehman found Lehman Brothers.
- **2003:** Riding a housing boom in the United States, Lehman acquires five mortgage lenders including subprime lender BNC Mortgage.
- **2007 (Feb):** Lehman's stock price hits a record high US$86.18, giving it a market capitalisation of nearly US$60 billion.

- **2007:** Lehman's mortgage-backed securities portfolio grows to $85 billion, about four times the shareholders' equity.
- **2007 (Aug):** The failure of two Bear Stearns hedge funds causes a sharp fall in the value of Lehman's stock. The company closes BNC Mortgage and lets 1,200 employees go.
- **2007 (Nov):** Lehman's stock rebounds thanks to a temporary boom in global equity markets, but the company fails to trim its mortgage portfolio.
- **2007 (Dec):** Lehman reports record annual net income of US$4.2 billion on revenue of US$19.3 billion.
- **2008 (Mar):** Lehman Brothers shares fall 48 per cent following the near-collapse of Bear Stearns, the second largest underwriter of mortgage-backed securities, that had been taken over by JP Morgan Chase.
- **2008 (June):** Lehman announces second-quarter losses of US$2.8 billion and is forced to sell US$6 billion worth of assets. It is the first quarterly loss for the company since it was spun-off from American Express in 1994.
- **2008 (9 Sept):** South Korean state-owned Korea Development Bank refuses to back Lehman and sets the stage for the ultimate fall of the investment bank.
- **2008 (10 Sept):** Lehman reports a loss of US$3.9 billion, a write-down of US$5.6 billion and a business restructuring plan.
- **2008 (13 Sept):** A takeover plan between Lehman, Barclays plc and Bank of America is unsuccessful.
- **2008 (15 Sept):** Lehman files for bankruptcy along with its 22 affiliates. The company has $639 billion in assets and $619 billion in debt. Its stock drops 93 per cent in a single day.
- **2008 (20 Sept):** Barclays plc's acquisition of Lehman's North American investment banking and capital markets business along with its New York headquarters and data centres for $1.35 billion is approved.
- **2008 (Oct):** Nomura, a Japanese brokerage, acquires most of Lehman's Asia Pacific franchises and part of its Europe and Middle Eastern division for $225 million and $2, hiring over 5,000 employees.

Response and Management

The crisis at Lehman spun out of control far too fast but at the heart of the problem was an inability to consider the liquidity implications of switching from a brokerage model to an investment bank one. The switch required a massive increase in liquidity risk but also made it more difficult for the bank to borrow capital and hedge risks. Perhaps these risks could have been avoided with more effective ALM.

When real estate prices in the US started to crash in 2006, reducing the value of Lehman's assets, the bank doubled up rather than scale back. In early 2007, shortly after it reported it highest profits ever—even as the prices of real estate were crumbling—the bank made it clear that the risks created by defaults in residential mortgages were contained and would not impact earnings at the firm.

At a time when most of their peers were reducing their exposure, Lehman decided to expand and acquire market share. It increased its credit risk, operational risk and market risk. In 2007, Lehman backed more mortgage-backed securities than any other firm. In the fourth quarter of the year, global equity markets briefly rebounded and so did fixed-income assets but Lehman did not take this opportunity to cut down on its mortgage portfolio.

More careful market analysis in response to the crisis could have shed some light on the risks the bank was taking but a widespread culture of growth, and pressure to expand at a rapid rate, overcame any considerations of risk. A high leverage ratio only amplified the problems—Lehman had assets of US$691 billion but only $22.5 billion in shareholder equity, which meant its liabilities were about $668.5 or 30 times its equity. A negative return of 4% would, at any time, have wiped out the equity. During boom times, this was no problem. When the bust happened, it was unsustainable.

Analysis

At its very core, ALM aims to manage the mismatches between assets and liabilities. These mismatches can be caused by changes in interest rates that can affect short-term liabilities and long-term assets, time differentials between assets and liabilities or the quality of assets, to name but three examples. Lehman was faced with a perfect storm of dropping asset quality, liabilities that came due and underperforming assets that led to an intolerable liquidity risk event. In other words, Lehman ran out of money to cover its liabilities.

The idea behind financial leverage is to take the proceeds of a borrowed loan and invest that at a higher rate of return—earning a spread. Most banks pay low rates on inter-bank market loans and invest the money by giving out loans to their clients or putting it into other vehicles at higher rates. Managing this spread effectively is a key goal of ALM. Lehman, unlike most banks, invested in mortgage-backed securities which became worthless. Instead of generating profits for Lehman (a positive spread) they started causing losses (a negative spread). And because the securities became virtually worthless, Lehman was left holding a big pile of debt (liabilities) with no assets to generate income to pay for them.

In its annual report for 2007, Lehman had identified a series of risks that threatened the business. One was market risk inherent in potential changes to the value of the various financial instruments it invested. A second was credit risk in the form of a counterparty that was unable to honour its debts. Third was operational risk in the event of losses caused from weak internal processes. Reputational risk was considered in the event that the public lost faith in the business. Liquidity risk was also considered as part of this exercise. Lehman's annual report thought it a possible risk that the bank would not be able to meet payment obligations, borrow funds in the market at a good price or fund commitments or liquidate assets. These risks, the bank made it clear, had to be carefully managed and balanced to ensure the continuation of operations.[7]

---

[7] Lehman Brothers (2008) 'Lehman Brothers Annual Report 2007'.

To do well in the ultra-competitive investment banking business, Lehman Brothers needed to show as much as 15% growth in annual revenues. This required even faster growth in the total capital base. To achieve this level of growth, the management changed the business strategy of the bank. It switched from being a brokerage, which has lower risk, into an investment bank. Rather than make money from transaction fees it sought to make money from long-term investments, particularly in real estate, leveraged loans and private equity. As part of this change, it got heavily involved in high-interest subprime loans and mortgages, which had proliferated thanks to a housing bubble through the first decade of the century.

Lehman was not the only bank to get involved in subprime loans or on derivative products intended to limit the risk associated with them. As housing prices rose and defaults stayed in check, many banks did very well by originating loans, turning them into securities called Residential Mortgage Backed Securities and selling those securities to other investors as profitable investments with little risk due to the independence of the loan takers and the rising real estate prices.

The structure started to crumble in 2006 when real estate prices crashed and interest rates started to climb. Default rates began to rise and investors came to realise that these mortgage-backed securities had more risk than was originally thought. Rating agencies started to downgrade them. Suddenly, Lehman (amongst other banks) was stuck with assets it could not sell, backed by mortgages that were in default and guaranteed by real estate that was dropping in value. Lehman had invested aggressively in these securities, much more so than any other investment bank. In the first quarter of 2008, Lehman reported losses of US$2.5 billion but the losses and the fact that the bank now had a weak balance sheet with illiquid assets were a terrible combination. Suddenly, all the risks that it had earlier considered as part of its risk control exercise were coming to the forefront. And the key risk was liquidity risk, with its assets losing value and an inability to sell those assets, Lehman found itself short of cash. In the second quarter of 2008, Lehman reported another loss of US$3.9 billion. By then, the market had little faith in Lehman and it became very hard for the bank to borrow enough to manage daily operations.

Bankruptcy became one of the few likely options for the bank. Negotiations for a sale with other banks failed and the US government chose not to intervene. On 15 September, 2008, Lehman Brothers filed for bankruptcy after 158 years. It was the largest bankruptcy in history and turned a credit crunch into a full blown financial crisis.

Lessons Learnt

A number of key lessons emerged from the bankruptcy at Lehman Brothers:

- Effective ALM is key to ensure steady but controlled growth and maintain a balance between assets and liabilities and secure the stability of a bank.
- Rapid expansion at the expense of risk control can have disastrous effects. It is one thing to consider risks, it is another to take those considerations into account when planning

future activity. Risk measurement and control efforts done simply as an exercise without a direct line to the decision makers are useless.

- It is also important to carefully valuate structured products. As the case at Lehman Brothers suggests, it can be difficult to determine the fair market price of some structured products, which makes risk management very difficult.

- It is key for management to have accurate daily views of the liquidity positions to be able to monitor them and react quickly to changes. This is key to ALM. In the case of Lehman, there were plenty of warning signs that liquidity was becoming a problem.

- The impact of a crisis such as the GFC on a bank's balance sheet can be long lasting, in this case, more than a decade.

- An appropriate amount of high quality liquid assets must be in place to be a safeguard against liquidity risk.

- Banks must be mindful of the complexity of correlation among risk factors. Credit risk (resulting from downgrade of sub-prime assets) can quickly turn into market risk (price drop of CDO). Concern that the bank may fail will lead to reputation risk. The resulting share price collapse and erosion of confidence in the repayment ability of the bank quickly impair the bank's ability to re-finance its short-term debt in the inter-bank market. Without HQLA to general cash, the bank will fail and liquidity risk is like the last straw on the camel's back.

- Liquidity stress test and contingency plan must be treated like a fire drill to ensure it is operational. There is no 'take two'.

Continental Illinois National Bank's Electronic Cash Out (1984)

The history of Continental Illinois National Bank and Trust Company can be traced back to two Chicago banks: the Commercial National Bank, founded during the American Civil War, and the Continental National Bank, founded in 1883. In 1910 the two banks merged to form the Continental & Commercial National Bank of Chicago with $175 million in deposits. In 1932 the bank's name was changed to the Continental Illinois National Bank & Trust Co. By the time it went insolvent, the bank had been in business for more than 124 years.

There are a number of factors that led to the failure of the regional giant; but at the heart of it all are gradual changes in management style that led to an unchecked increase in risk appetite without a commensurate consideration of risk.

During the two decades before its default, Continental Illinois was focused on growth, with a particular focus on international expansion. The bank started pursuing an aggressive growth strategy in the late 1970s and, by 1981, it was the largest commercial and industrial (C&I) lender in the United States. Continental had 57 offices in 14 states and 29 foreign countries.

Between 1976 and 1981, Continental Illinois's C&I lending jumped from approximately US$5 billion to more than US$14 billion and total assets grew from US$21.5 billion to US$45 billion. The bank's loans-to-assets ratio increased from 57.9 per cent in 1977 to 68.8 per cent by year-end 1981. The bank's return on assets (year-end net income divided by year-end assets) stayed at 0.5% during the same period while the return on equity (year-end net income divided by year-end equity) was 14.4%. Due to the aggressive pursuit in C&I lending, Continental's retail banking business and total core deposits remained relatively small. The bank sustained itself on federal funds and large certificates of deposits (CDs) purchased in the secondary market.

Problems started emerging when Oklahoma City's Penn Square Bank failed as a result of irresponsible lending practices in connection with the sale of well over US$1 billion in 'loan participations' to other banks throughout the US. Continental had purchased almost US$1 billion in energy-related loans from Penn Square. With Penn Square's default, Continental's earnings and reputation were dragged down. Clearly the loans were poorly underwritten—evidence that Continental had not conducted appropriate due diligence on the loans it had purchased.

The situation became worse as more evidence of improper checks and balances and even conflicts of interest surfaced. When Continental's internal auditors visited Penn Square in December 1981, they found evidence of US$565,000 in personal loans from Penn Square to John Lytle, the officer at Continental who was responsible for acquiring the Oklahoma City bank's loans. In 1982, stock analysts downgraded the earnings estimates on Continental Illinois, sending the bank's share price sharply down by approximately 62% from its peak just a year earlier. Credit rating agencies started to downgrade the bank's credit and debt ratings.

By 1983, two of the largest majority shareholders of Continental had sold all their stock. The scale of the problem was exacerbated when rumours started to circulate that Continental bank would fail. Large foreign depositors panicked, triggering a high-speed electronic deposit run in May 1984. That month, banks from all over the world including the Netherlands, West Germany, Switzerland and Japan increased the interest rates they changed on loans to Continental. And the problems grew even worse when Reuters, the British news wire, published a story that a Japanese bank was considering buying Continental. Soon after the story was distributed, Japanese and European money started pulling out at an alarming speed.

By May 19, the bank saw US$6 billion of foreign money withdrawn from its balance sheet. In the US, the Chicago Board of Trade Clearing Corporation withdrew another US$50 million on May 9. By May 11, Continental's borrowings at the discount window of the Federal Reserve Bank to make up for its lost deposits had reached $3.6 billion.[8]

---

[8] FDIC, https://www.fdic.gov/bank/historical/managing/history2-04.pdf.

Chronology

The events surrounding the fall of Continental evolved as follows.

- **1910:** Commercial National Bank and the Continental National Bank merge to create a single entity with US$175 million in deposits.
- **1932:** Name changed to the Continental Illinois National Bank & Trust Co.
- **1973:** Continental embarks on an aggressive assault on selected segments of the banking market. The bank starts to rapidly build up its consumer loan portfolio.
- **Mid-1970s:** Continental takes a hit from the collapse of the real estate investment trust industry. However, management handles this particular risk event well and recovers from the problems caused by the fall of the real estate market with greater success than most other large banks.
- **1974:** Continental Illinois goes through a period of rapid growth in assets, greater specialisation in lending towards the energy sector and corporate lending more broadly. Continental's assets start growing an average of more than 13% per year. By the end of 1979, the bank's mortgage and real estate portfolio grows from US$997 million to approximately US$2.3 billion. Meanwhile, the Office of the Comptroller of the Currency's (OCC) assessment of Continental's management and its performance during eight examinations conducted during the period between 1974 and 1981 are favourable.
- **1976:** Concerns are raised by OCC examiners over the bank's liquidity position and its reliance on Fed Funds, foreign deposits and negotiable CDs.
- **1977:** An examination in the summer of 1977 shows that Continental Illinois had improved its liquidity position and enhanced its monitoring systems. OCC examiners conclude that its funding and control concerns were being adequately monitored by the bank.
- **1980:** Continental Illinois is able to achieve one of the best and most consistent performance records of any large bank in the US.
- **1981:** Continental Illinois becomes the sixth largest US bank with assets worth US$45.1 billion and 12,000 employees. By year-end 1981, the bank's net income rises rapidly before peaking at US$236 million. By 1981, energy loans represent 20% of Continental's total loans and leases and 47% of its total C&I loans. Continental has more than $6.7 billion in oil and gas loans outstanding.
- **1981 (Dec):** An audit by the OCC uncovers US$565,000 in personal loans from Penn Square to John R. Lytle, manager of Continental Illinois's Mid-Continent Division of the Oil and Gas Group and the officer responsible for the acquisition of Penn Square loans. No action is taken by Continental Illinois to remove Lytle until May 1982.
- **1982 (5 July):** The failure of Penn Square Bank leads to a run on Continental Illinois. Continental Illinois loses 40% of its domestic funding.

- **1982:** Nonperforming assets, totalling US$643 million at the end of 1981, grow to US$844 million at the end of the first quarter of 1982.
- **1982 (June):** Loans purchased from Penn Square average less than 3% of Continental Illinois' total loans over the previous two and a half years but account for 41% of the bank's losses between June 1981 and June 1982. Penn Square loans have thus far resulted in nearly US$500 million in loan losses for Continental Illinois.
- **1984 (9 May):** A run on Continental Illinois assets begins in Tokyo, with investors looking to pull their deposits out or to sell their investments.
- **1984 (14 May):** A group of 16 banks provide Continental Illinois with a 30-day line of credit of US$4.5 billion.
- **1984 (17 May):** Regulators announce an interim assistance package of unprecedented size, a package that in the end tops US$13.5 billion.
- **1984 (26 Sept):** The Federal Deposit Insurance Corporation (FDIC) implements a restructuring process that effectively nationalises Continental Illinois.
- **1991:** The FDIC sells the last of its equity stake in Continental Illinois, seven years after the bank's collapse.

Response and Management

In May 1984 Continental Illinois became insolvent almost directly as a result of a series of bad loans purchased from the failed Penn Square Bank. The bad decision to add Penn's large portfolio of loans to Continental Illinois's balance sheet was exacerbated by a run on the bank. Scared by the potential fallout of such a large number of bad loans, investors withdrew as much as US$10 billion worth of deposits in early May 1984. The sheer size of the bank run went well beyond what both the bank's risk managers and regulators had ever expected.

The problem for regulators was the sheer size of Continental Illinois, which made the bank systemically important. The fear—one that would be revisited during multiple crises years later—was that the failure of such a large financial institution would have significant ramifications throughout the economy. In the end, regulators decided that letting the bank fail was simply not an acceptable option.

According to documents from the FDIC, federal agencies agreed that Continental Illinois' failure would threaten the immediate health of many smaller banks whose deposits it held. Such an outcome would have a multiplier effect, impacting the economy of the region and even the country. The FDIC feared a failure could cause widespread financial trouble and instability. As a result, it put together a US$4.5 billion rescue package aimed at recapitalising the bank in the wake of a giant bank run.

Continental's bank crisis was resolved through open bank assistance on 17 May, 1984. The resolution involved a two-step process. The first step was an interim financial assistance package followed by a more permanent recapitalisation after four months. The federal government intervened with a huge bailout of US$4.5 billion of new capital for the bank as well as US$8 billion in emergency loans. New management was also put in place as the entire board of directors and top management were removed. Unfortunately, both directors and top managers were virtually wiped out. On the other hand, holding-company bondholders were protected from the failure as were hundreds of thousands of direct and indirect depositors.

In the end, however, the US federal government was left in effective control of roughly 80% of the company's shares and with a right to obtain the remainder if the size of the rescue exceeded certain thresholds. The government had sought out a private sector partner for the bailout but could not find any for more than two months.

It was not until a decade later, in 1994, that Bank of America acquired Continental Illinois after the federal government started a gradual disposal of its ownership interest in the once-respected bank.

Analysis

Continental had long been a conservative bank, but that changed when management decided to pursue an aggressive growth strategy in the mid-1970s. In implementing this strategy, Continental's opportunities for domestic growth were sharply constrained by state laws which, at the time, prohibited interstate banking and limited the opening of in-state branches, according to Federal Reserve economist Tara Rice, and the Morningstar equity analyst, Erin Davis.

In order to implement its growth strategy, Continental Illinois increased its domestic commercial and industrial lending by 180% between 1976 and 1981, largely through aggressively competing in the national commercial lending market in terms of loan rates and quality. In turn, to fund this rapid growth in lending, Continental Illinois increasingly resorted to buying federal funds and issuing CDs, backed by increasingly smaller per centages of reserve capital. The risks in Continental Illinois's rapid growth strategy first became apparent in late 1981 with notable deterioration in its corporate loan portfolio.

Continental was also exposed to risky debt from less developed countries, mostly in Latin America, which started showing weakness in 1982 as a prelude to a large crisis throughout the region. Nevertheless, as other banks were being downgraded, Continental Illinois retained its AAA rating from Fitch Ratings, even as late as March 1982. However, in July 1982, market perception of Continental Illinois' condition deteriorated abruptly after Penn Square went bankrupt. Continental Illinois had recently acquired a large group of loans from Penn Square with only limited due diligence.

The loans that Continental Illinois had acquired from Penn Square were generally linked to the oil and gas market. In the late 1970s there had been a sharp upward spike in oil prices, which led to rapid growth in opportunities to lend in the oil-producing states, one of them Oklahoma. Penn Square, which was based in Oklahoma, had aggressively exploited these opportunities even when doing so meant ignoring the basics of credit risk management.[9] The volume of loans generated by Penn Square far exceeded its capacity to fund

---

[9] *Wall Street Journal* reporter Phillip Zweig (1985) documents numerous violations of good lending practice. My favourite is an 'innovation' of Penn Square that Zweig (page 120) says 'could have been called the "negotiable cocktail napkin"'.

them or the reserves it held, so the bank sold loan participations to other banks, with Continental Illinois being one of the largest buyers.

By the beginning of the next decade, Penn Square's weak risk control led to the bank's failure and market participants started to quickly reevaluate the value of those loan participations and the health of banks with significant exposures to them. As a result, Continental Illinois, one of the largest holders, found its access to domestic funding markets sharply impaired. The bank then had to start paying higher rates of interest for short-term funding from foreign money markets, a situation that quickly became untenable as the mismatch between tenors in assets and liabilities spiralled out of control. A bank run caused by the sudden fear of failure only sped up the inevitable conclusion as the financial health of the bank continued to deteriorate through 1983 and into 1984.[10]

Lessons Learnt

A number of lessons can be learnt from the fall of Continental Illinois:

- For banks, a key lesson from the fall of Continental Illinois was the need to step up risk controls and the importance of proper capitalisation, not only to back deposits but also derivatives such as large loan packages. In broad strokes, the market risk and liquidity risk associated with the package of loans that Continental Illinois bought from Penn Square were not considered in detail.
- Although Continental Illinois failed, the methods used by regulators in the Continental Illinois transaction to deal with the problem worked reasonably well. The Continental resolution went on to become one of the go-to approaches for the FDIC to deal with future bank crises.
- The problems at Continental Illinois underlined some of the difficulties the FDIC has when dealing with large bank failures. Permanent direct assistance is generally rejected for several reasons. First, there is generally insufficient knowledge of the workings of a particular institution and the ultimate size of the liabilities. Second, time is a factor, particularly the time it takes to resolve gargantuan legal and accounting problems.
- There were two primary concerns that emerged from the Continental Illinois transaction. The first was the idea that would later become prominent: of banks that are 'too big to fail'. The second was whether the FDIC's protection of creditors other than insured depositors eroded market discipline in a way that intensified banking problems in later years.[11] One concern that remained is the need for a metric for what constitutes 'too big'.
- Ultimately, the decision on whether to bail out a bank is not just about the direct fallout from its failure but also on the potential indirect consequences for the stability of funding at other associated banks and even private depositors.

---

[10]Federal Reserve Bank of Atlanta, https://www.frbatlanta.org/cenfis/publications/notesfromthevault/1604#src4.

[11]FDIC, https://www.fdic.gov/bank/historical/managing/history2-04.pdf.

Bank of New England's Silent Run (1991)

The Bank of New England Corporation (BNE Corp) was formed as the first interstate regional bank in the US as a result of a merger in 1985 between the Bank of New England Corporation and Connecticut Bank & Trust Company (CB&T). The latter was the older of the two, tracing back to 1792 under the name of Union Bank of New London.

The Boston-based BNE Corp was one of the largest financial groups in the state of Massachusetts, owning nine banks with 470 branches and 17 other companies that provided different financial services including consumer banking, wholesale banking and operational services such as payroll, mutual funds and data processing. After the merger, BNE Corp did very well by riding the economic boom in the north-east of the US and through multiple acquisitions. The region's real estate prices and the economy in the north-east grew by nearly 20% per year for several years. The banking group grew larger at a very rapid pace.

However, by 1990, value of real estate began to fall and vacancy rates for both residential and commercial properties started rising. That was when the problems emerged at Bank of New England (BNE). In 1989, BNE announced a US$1.23 billion loss for the fourth quarter of the year. By September 1990 the local economy had been faltering for several months and almost half the loans BNE had extended for construction projects were written off as delinquent. With the number of bad loans compounding, BNE set aside reserves to cover loan losses that amounted to about US$650 million in 1990. And BNE was not the only bank in the region with problems. As many as 40% of all banks in the region reported negative income in 1990.

When BNE Corp's problems came to light, the blame fell largely on CEO Walter J. Connolly Jr., who had led the group through an acquisition binge in an effort to drive growth. Under his leadership the bank was pushed further into the real estate business in the second half of the 1980s.

On 6 January, 1991, BNE, and its two sister banks, CB&T, and Maine National Bank (MNB) failed. All three banks were owned by BNE Corp. The aim of the ultimate resolution was to protect all depositors, not just those affiliated with BNE Corp.

At the time of its failure BNE was the 33rd largest bank in the US and CB&T was the largest bank in the state of Connecticut. Along with sister bank MNB, the three banks had US$21.8 billion in total assets and operated 117 branches in New England. They held more than US$19 billion in deposits when all three banks defaulted on their obligations.

Chronology

The events surrounding the fall of BNE transpired as follows.

- **1792:** CBT, better known as Connecticut Bank and Trust Company, is incorporated in 1792 as Union Bank of New London.

- **1831:** Merchants Bank, Bank of New England's earliest predecessor, is granted a state charter in Massachusetts.
- **1863:** The US Congress passes the National Banking Act.
- **1985:** BNE Corp is created from merger of Bank of New England Corporation and CBT Corporation, another bank holding company from Connecticut. It is the first interstate regional bank holding company.
- **1988:** BNE Corp lists on the New York Stock Exchange under the symbol of NEB.
- **1989:** CEO Walter Connolly resigns. The FDIC issues a cease and desist order to the bank to restrain its aggressive lending practices.
- **1990:** BNE swings from a US$74 million profit in 1989 to a US$1.2 billion loss in 1990. The loss is attributed to poor investments in the real estate market. Also, in part, due to a larger savings and loan crisis that overtakes the banking industry at the time. Poor investments are a result of CEO Walter Connolly's aggressive growth and acquisition strategy throughout the mid-1980s. Lending problems emerge in early 1990 when, after a bank examination, BNE Corp announces a $1.23 billion loss for the fourth quarter of 1989. Real estate values in the north-east are falling. Vacancy rates for residential and commercial properties are rising.
- **1990 (Feb and Apr):** A new management team, headed by Lawrence K. Fish, is installed at BNE Corp.
- **1990 (Sept):** Almost half the loans BNE has made for construction projects and nearly 20% of its mortgage loans for commercial project are delinquent.
- **1991 (4 Jan):** BNE Corp indicates that it has lost up to US$450 million in the fourth quarter of 1990, mostly as a result of losses on its delinquent real estate loans.
- **1991 (6 Jan):** The OCC closes both BNE and CB&T. The FDIC exercises a cross guarantee authority and orders the payment of $1,015,000 by the affiliated MNB (Maine National Bank).
- **1991 (7 Jan):** FDIC creates three bridge banks: New Bank of New England, New Connecticut Bank & Trust Company, New Maine National Bank, and opens them for business on January 7.
- **1991 (22 Apr):** The FDIC board of directors, Fleet and Norstar Financial Group Inc., a Rhode Island banking company, along with Kohlberg, Kravis, Roberts & Company agree to buy the failed BNE and the two affiliated banks, CB&T and MNB.

Response and Management

In response to the emerging problems, in January 1991 the FDIC seized BNE and placed it into Chapter 7 bankruptcy liquidation. The Office of the Comptroller of the Currency (OCC) closed both BNE and CB&T on Sunday, 6 January, 1991 and appointed the FDIC as receiver. The FDIC used its cross guarantee assessment authority to assess MNB for the FDIC's cost associated with the BNE failure. As part of the transaction, the FDIC injected $750 million of capital into bridge banks.

The FDIC then went on to create three bridge banks: New Bank of New England (New BNE), with assets of approximately $8 billion; New Connecticut Bank & Trust (New CB&T) with assets of approximately $6.4 billion, and New Maine National Bank (New MNB) with assets of approximately $800 million. All deposits from the previous banks were transferred to the bridge banks.

Despite efforts to restore the financial health of the company, such as selling off the credit card unit to Citigroup and laying off 5,600 employees, BNE's losses were proving too large. The Federal Reserve's Boston branch loaned the bank another $478 million as temporary financing, but real estate related losses for the year of nearly US$6 billion over-whelmed the bank's solvency. Part of the problem involved large loans made between bank entities in the holding group that distorted financial results, as well as embezzlement by a vice-president of the bank, which was discovered at the height of the crisis in late 1990.

In order to limit an ongoing run on the bank, which could be triggered once customers start panicking about the safety of their deposits, the FDIC fully protected all deposits of all three failed banks, including deposits exceeding the US$100,000 insurance limit. The total cost of the bailout was an estimated at US$2.3 billion. Even after the assurance, US$1.5 billion dollars were withdrawn from the bank.

The problem with BNE, as with most banks, is that it did not have anywhere near enough reserves to cover such large and rapid withdrawals. BNE was a prime example of a bank facing a liquidity risk event as loans, which are a bank's key asset, stop performing and become liabilities. Most banks in the north-eastern region had already ceased making commercial real estate loans and commercial and industrial loans or had at least pulled back significantly at the first sign of trouble in the market. Not so with BNE.

Eventually, however, even BNE stopped lending. However, evidence suggests that most decisions to discontinue lending were initiated by bank management rather than supervisory authorities. The seriousness of the problems became apparent to supervisors only gradually, in part because examinations of some banks focused more on policies than on detailed review of credit quality and lending terms.

Analysis

BNE wasn't alone in the downward spiral. Commercial real estate loans were the dominant factor in the majority of the bank failures in New England at the time. Of the 62 banks in existence before 1984 that failed from 1989 to 1992, commercial real estate loans were the dominant factor in 58 failures. Commercial real estate loans exceeded 30% of assets in 47 of the 62 established banks in one study and were higher than 20% of assets in all but four. Prior to 1984, commercial real estate loans seldom exceeded 20% of assets in any financial institution.

BNE did react appropriately when it finally recognised the extent and nature of the problems it faced. However, its actions came too late to prevent a failure. Indirect evidence shows that the real estate loan problems in New England during this period were based almost entirely on construction and development lending and the resulting damage to the economics of existing commercial properties.[12]

Lessons Learnt

A number of lessons can be learnt from the fall of BNE:

- Risk diversification is key. BNE lent too much, too aggressively, too quickly for a number of years in a single sector and was powerless to address a collapse in its key market.
- Greater supervisory oversight could have helped. At the time regulators found the quality of BNE's loans to be poor and the record keeping inadequate. Better systems for internal controls could also have limited a lot of the problems.
- Fresh injections of capital can help, but only if they are timely.

Summary

- Royal Bank of Scotland, one of the best known banks in the United Kingdom, failed mandatory stress tests in 2016, eight years after almost going bust as a result of the Global Financial Crisis.
- Between 2006 and 2008, the bank led by CEO Sir Fred Goodwin relied for much of its growth on the Global Banking & Markets (GBM) and UK Corporate Banking operations. GBM made up half of the bank's assets by 2008. Those two operations grew in size from GBP500bn to GBP830bn in those two years alone.
- In a controversial acquisition in 2007, RBS acquired the giant Dutch bank ABN for GBP1.9trn. Afterwards, the balance sheet of the GBM alone exploded to GBP1.2trn with 100-times leverage.
- At the end of 2008, RBS almost failed. No regulatory wrongdoing was found but the Bank of England had to provide capital for the bank to survive. By 2008, UK taxpayers had taken a 78.3% stake in the bank.
- Lehman Brothers, the bank at the heart of the largest bank failure in history, started in 1850 as a grocery story. It expanded enormously over the next century and a half until its collapse in 2008.
- Lehman's assets were unbalanced, with the bank having invested enormously in mortgage backed securities that lost much of their value through 2007 and 2008, creating a giant mismatch between assets and liabilities. In effect, the bank's assets became worthless while their liabilities remained intact.

---

[12]'Evidence on the Relative Contributions of Commercial and Residential Real Estate to New England Bank Credit Problems.'

- At its very core, ALM aims to eliminate mismatches between assets and liabilities. Lehman was faced with a perfect storm of dropping asset quality, liabilities that came due and underperforming assets that led to an intolerable liquidity risk event. In other words, Lehman ran out of money to cover its liabilities. Poor risk controls likely led to this situation.
- With a history dating back to 1883, Continental Illinois National Bank & Trust Co. went insolvent in 1984.
- Between 1976 and 1981, Continental's commercial and industrial lending jumped from approximately US$5 billion to more than US$14 billion and total assets grew from US$21.5 billion to US$45 billion. The bank's loans-to-assets ratio increased from 57.9 per cent in 1977 to 68.8 per cent by year-end 1981.
- Continental Illinois bought a large package of loans from Penn Square Bank that were broadly linked to oil development in Oklahoma. When the oil market crashed, those loans created a crisis of confidence in Continental Illinois. Domestic and foreign investors started cashing out to the tune of US$6 billion by May 1984.
- Believing the bank was too big to fail, regulators stepped in with a US$4.5 billion bailout that left the US federal government in control of the bank. A decade later, Bank of America acquired the ownership interest held by the government.
- The Bank of New England Corp traced its history back to 1792. It failed in 1991.
- Based in Boston, BNE Corp was a diversified financial group with nine banks, 17 other companies and 470 branches. They grew rapidly through the 1980s by focusing on real estate loans, particularly for construction in the north-east of the US. By 1991, as many as 30% of its loans were in this one sector. When real estate started crashing in the region, so did BNE.
- A silent bank run on the bank led to withdrawals worth US$1.5 billion in rapid succession, even though the FDIC had fully protected deposits as part of a US$2.3 billion bailout.
- BNE was too slow to react to the crash of the real estate market and so were regulators, who did not consider the dangers of such a large proportion of loans in a single sector.

Key Terms

Asset and liability management (ALM)
Asset and Liability Management
    Committee (ALCO)
Bank of England (BoE)
Bank of New England Corporation (BNE)
Certificates of deposit (CDs)
Chicago Board of Trade Clearing
    Corporation

Commercial National Bank
Common Equity Tier 1 (CET1) ratio
Connecticut Bank & Trust Company
    (CB&T)
Continental Illinois National Bank
Continental National Bank
Federal Deposit Insurance Corporation
Federal Reserve Bank

Financial Services Authority (FSA)

Global Financial Crisis (GFC)

Lehman Brothers

Liquidity risk

Loan participations

Loans-to-assets ratio

Maine National Bank

Market risk

Mortgage-backed securities

New Bank of New England

New Connecticut Bank & Trust

New Maine National Bank

Non-performing assets (NPA)

Office of the Comptroller of the Currency

Penn Square Bank

Return on assets

Return on equity

Royal Bank of Scotland (RBS)

Subprime crisis

Union Bank of New London

Walter Connolly

Review Questions

1. Describe the events that led to the Royal Bank of Scotland requiring a bailout from UK taxpayers after the Global Financial Crisis? Why was it significant that the bank failed to pass stress tests in 2016, almost eight years later?
2. Discuss why the bankruptcy of Lehman Brothers in 2008 was felt around the world. What was, from your point of view, the most significant factor that led to the failure of such a venerable institution?
3. How did Bank of New England end up with such a large concentration of loans in a single sector? What would you, as a risk manager, consider danger signs?
4. Discuss the regulatory response to the BNE failure. Was it timely? Appropriate? Why?

Further Reading

Carlson, Mark and Rose, Jonathan. 'Can a Bank Run Be Stopped? Government Guarantees and the Run on Continental Illinois'. Bank for International Settlements. March 2016. http://www.bis.org/publ/work554.pdf.

Fraser, Ian. *Shredded: The Rise and Fall of the Royal Bank of Scotland*. Edinburgh: Birlinn. 2014.

Lohr, Steve. 'When a Big Bank Went Under, US Presence Stemmed the Panic.' *New York Times*. 18 February 1991. http://www.nytimes.com/1991/02/18/business/when-a-bigbank-went-under-us-presence-stemmed-the-panic.html?pagewanted=all.

McCollorn, James (1987) *The Continental affair: The rise and fall of the Continental Illinois Bank*. New York: Mead Dodd.

McDonald, Lawrence and Robinson, Patrick. *A Colossal Failure of Common Sense: The Inside Story of the Collapse of Lehman Brothers*. US: Crown Publishing Group. 2009.

Wall, Larry D. 'Ending Too Big to Fail: Lessons from Continental Illinois'. Center for Financial Innovation and Stability. April 2016 https://www.frbatlanta.org/cenfis/publications/notesfromthevault/1604.

Principles for Sound Liquidity Risk Management and Supervision

(Published by BIS Basel Committee on Banking Supervision, September 2008)

Principle 1: A bank is responsible for the sound management of liquidity risk. A bank should establish a robust liquidity risk management framework that ensures it maintains sufficient liquidity, including a cushion of unencumbered, high quality liquid assets, to withstand a range of stress events, including those involving the loss or impairment of both unsecured and secured funding sources. Supervisors should assess the adequacy of both a bank's liquidity risk management framework and its liquidity position and should take prompt action if a bank is deficient in either area in order to protect depositors and to limit potential damage to the financial system.

Governance of Liquidity Risk Management

Principle 2: A bank should clearly articulate a liquidity risk tolerance that is appropriate for its business strategy and its role in the financial system.

    Principle 3: Senior management should develop a strategy, policies and practices to manage liquidity risk in accordance with the risk tolerance and to ensure that the bank maintains sufficient liquidity. Senior management should continuously review information on the bank's liquidity developments and report to the board of directors on a regular basis. A bank's board of directors should review and approve the strategy, policies and practices related to the management of liquidity at least annually and ensure that senior management manages liquidity risk effectively.

    Principle 4: A bank should incorporate liquidity costs, benefits and risks in the internal pricing, performance measurement and new product approval process for all significant business activities (both on- and off-balance-sheet), thereby aligning the risk-taking incentives of individual business lines with the liquidity risk exposures their activities create for the bank as a whole.

Measurement and Management of Liquidity Risk

Principle 5: A bank should have a sound process for identifying, measuring, monitoring and controlling liquidity risk. This process should include a robust framework for comprehensively projecting cash flows arising from assets, liabilities and off-balance-sheet items over an appropriate set of time horizons.

    Principle 6: A bank should actively monitor and control liquidity risk exposures and funding needs within and across legal entities, business lines and currencies, taking into account legal, regulatory and operational limitations to the transferability of liquidity.

    Principle 7: A bank should establish a funding strategy that provides effective diversification in the sources and tenor of funding. It should maintain an ongoing presence in its chosen funding markets and strong relationships with funds providers to promote effective diversification of funding sources. A bank should regularly gauge its capacity to raise funds quickly from each source. It should identify the main factors that affect its ability to raise funds and monitor those factors closely to ensure that estimates of fund raising capacity remain valid.

Principle 8: A bank should actively manage its intraday liquidity positions and risks to meet payment and settlement obligations on a timely basis under both normal and stressed conditions and thus contribute to the smooth functioning of payment and settlement systems.

Principle 9: A bank should actively manage its collateral positions, differentiating between encumbered and unencumbered assets. A bank should monitor the legal entity and physical location where collateral is held and how it may be mobilised in a timely manner.

Principle 10: A bank should conduct stress tests on a regular basis for a variety of short-term and protracted institution-specific and market-wide stress scenarios (individually and in combination) to identify sources of potential liquidity strain and to ensure that current exposures remain in accordance with a bank's established liquidity risk tolerance. A bank should use stress test outcomes to adjust its liquidity risk management strategies, policies, and positions and to develop effective contingency plans.

Principle 11: A bank should have a formal contingency funding plan (CFP) that clearly sets out the strategies for addressing liquidity shortfalls in emergency situations. A CFP should outline policies to manage a range of stress environments, establish clear lines of responsibility, include clear invocation and escalation procedures and be regularly tested and updated to ensure that it is operationally robust.

Principle 12: A bank should maintain a cushion of unencumbered, high quality liquid assets to be held as insurance against a range of liquidity stress scenarios, including those that involve the loss or impairment of unsecured and typically available secured funding sources. There should be no legal, regulatory or operational impediment to using these assets to obtain funding.

Public Disclosure

Principle 13: A bank should publicly disclose information on a regular basis that enables market participants to make an informed judgement about the soundness of its liquidity risk management framework and liquidity position.

The Role of Supervisors

Principle 14: Supervisors should regularly perform a comprehensive assessment of a bank's overall liquidity risk management framework and liquidity position to determine whether they deliver an adequate level of resilience to liquidity stress given the bank's role in the financial system.

Principle 15: Supervisors should supplement their regular assessments of a bank's liquidity risk management framework and liquidity position by monitoring a combination of internal reports, prudential reports and market information.

Principle 16: Supervisors should intervene to require effective and timely remedial action by a bank to address deficiencies in its liquidity risk management processes or liquidity position.

Principle 17: Supervisors should communicate with other supervisors and public authorities, such as central banks, both within and across national borders, to facilitate effective cooperation regarding the supervision and oversight of liquidity risk management. Communication should occur regularly during normal times, with the nature and frequency of the information sharing increasing as appropriate during times of stress.

Index